Diversity:
Mestizos, Latinos and the Promise of Possibilities

Amardo Rodríguez

Floricanto Press

Copyright © 2007 by Amardo Rodríguez.
Copyright © 2007 of this edition by Floricanto Press.

All rights reserved. Except for brief passages quoted in a review, no part of this book may be reproduced in any form, by photostat, microfilm, xerography, electronic and digital reproduction, or placed in the Internet, or any other means, or incorporated into any information retrieval system, electronic, or mechanical, without written permission of the publisher.
ISBN: 978-0-915745-92-0
Floricanto Press
650 Castro Street, Suite 120-331
Mountain View, California 94041-2055
www. floricantopress. com

Diversity

For My Beloved Grandfather
Domingo Boneo

Table of Contents

Prologue 9
I.   Culture To Culturing 12
The Relation Between Ambiguity and Meaning 14
Rhythms, Tensions, and Meanings 18
New Vistas and New Possibilities 24
Final Thoughts 26
II.   Spanglish And The Quest For Possibility 28
Check Miscellaneous 31
Spanglish and the Critics 35
Final Thoughts 42
III.   The Challenge of The New Mestizas 44
On The Origins Of Being Other 46
The Power of Illusions 50
Our Storied Worlds 54
Final Thoughts 55
IV.   Our Deep Prejudices 57
Crime & Punishment 62
Crimes of Hate 64

Legitimizing The Status Quo	66
Love & Hate	69
Final Thoughts	73
V. On Differences & Diversity	76
Diversity As A Verb	78
Diversity, Time & Space	81
Literality Promotes Homogeneity	82
VI. The New Politics	94
Identity & Meaning	97
Final Thoughts	100
VII. Communion	102
On Inclusion and Exclusion	105
The Perils Of Global Capitalism	113
Forging A New Understanding Of Progress	116
The Origins of Mutuality	120
Democracy and Diversity	122
VIII. On The Challenge of Diversity: A Case Study	126
Protests, Petitions, and Vigils	129
Final Thoughts	141
Epilogue	143
References	146

Prologue

In a previous book, *Diversity As Liberation (II): Introducing A New Understanding of Diversity*, I argued for an emergent understanding of diversity that foregrounds notions of union, evolution, and communion. Diversity is about the communion of differences. It is about the evolution of new ways of experiencing and understanding the world through our forging of communion with each other and the world. Communion reflects the blossoming of our moral, existential, and spiritual strives. Such strives uniquely reflect our capacity to construct deep and complex relations with the world, and through the evolution of such relations hierarchy devolves. Diversity is therefore an expression of liberation. Its evolution reflects the end of hierarchy. No doubt, this emergent understanding of diversity is unequivocally political. It politicizes us. In *Diversity As Liberation* I sought to show how diversity deligitimizes the status quo. I also sought to show how diversity as communion deepens our understanding of the human condition and, in so doing, releases us of commonly held fears and myths of the human condition that the status quo uses to limit the evolution of new and different ways of experiencing and understanding the world. Diversity as communion renews our hope in our potentiality to create more just and humane worlds.

In this present book I contend that identity politics masks the machinations of domination and oppression. Domination constitutes arrangements and practices that systematically block the evolution of our moral, existential, and spiritual strives. Identity politics shifts attention away from the structural forces that undergird modern society that make for domination and oppression. Its fixation with discrimination deflects attention from the origins of oppression, and its goal to end bigotry and discrimination poses no threat to the status quo. I also contend that identity politics calls us to risk no life. It depoliticizes us. It poses no threat to the status quo and thereby legitimizes and even protects our deep biases and prejudices from any kind of serious scrutiny.

I also contend that identity politics trivializes our understanding of diversity. Diversity is reduced to differences. This understanding of diversity poses no threat to the status quo. We can have differences but no diversity. In such cases, as is the norm, diversity is reduced to plurality. We assume that diversity merely demands bringing *differences* to the equation. Further, identity politics sustains assumptions, fears, beliefs, and truths of human beings of the world that block any serious consideration of the possibility of a society devoid of hierarchy. Foremost among such assumptions and beliefs is the notion that human beings possess a natural proclivity for chaos and devolution. Supposedly, human beings are by nature beasts; accordingly, hierarchy is supposedly vital for the evolution of the good society. In this way, identity politics further legitimizes our distrust and suspicion of the human condition. Most of all, I contend that identity politics undermines our understanding of what being human means and, in so doing, blocks the evolution of new vistas to look at what being human means. In other words, this politics obstructs the evolution of any potentially new politics that possibly transcends notions of domination and exploitation. It bounds us to a certain way of being and experiencing the world. In identity politics, toleration of our differences is supposedly the best that can be had. In *Diversity As Liberation*, I argued that toleration as a political ambition is morally, politically, and theoretically bankrupt. In fact, even the most vociferous proponents of toleration admit that toleration is laden with contractions.

I will give no serious consideration to any argument that assumes that human beings are morally unequal. That is, I will chase no shadows. The concept of equality only has purchase in a worldview with a deep hierarchical ethos. I enter this project on the assumption that human beings will always be different but morally equal as regards our potentiality to form deep and complex relations with each other and the world. We are all *blessed* with a boundless potentiality that moves and sustains all of the world and all of the heavens. It is our moral and spiritual obligation to help each other harness this potentiality so as to bring completion to the world and to ourselves. We are thereby obligated to promote union and communion rather than separation and fragmentation. It is through union and communion our redemption rests. Discrimination is also a shadow. Thus I have no intention of arguing why discrimination violates the natural order of the world.

In this book I offer the beginnings of what I will refer to as a new politics of communion. We no doubt need a new diversity politics to deal with the emerging global capitalism forces that are heightening the forces of domination and oppression. I discuss the discursive, communicative, and performative practices that come with this new politics. I also discuss the many obstacles that attend to the evolution of this new politics.

I
Culture To Culturing

An emergent view in intercultural communication theory is challenging the commonly held view that cultures are stable and homogenous (Belay, 1993; Casmir, 1993; Dervin, 1991; Martin & Nakayama, 1999; McPhail, 1996; Rodriguez, 2003; Said, 2000; Shuter, 1993; Starosta, 1991). The common criticism is that we are masking the many points of conflict, dissent, and diversity that permeate all cultures and, in so doing, masking the full complexity that cultures possess and even create. More importantly, such masking, in exaggerating (really distorting) our perceptions of homogeneity and stability, forces us to adopt dichotomous stances that stop us from "moving toward multiple perspectives that might inform each other in a dialogue of differences" (Dervin, 1991, p. 50). As Said (2001) notes, "There isn't a single Islam: there are Islams, just as there are Americas. This diversity is true of all traditions, religions or nations even though some of their adherents have futilely tried to draw boundaries around themselves and pin their creeds down neatly." We are demanding more complex understandings of how we constitute cultures so as to reflect and speak better to the complexity, discontinuity, and diversity that all cultures inherently possess and to devise means to have more constructive and nonviolent ways to deal with our rich and infinite differences. We are therefore more and more writing about *placing* and *racing* and *differencing* instead of ethnicity and race and difference so as to afford a more heuristic understanding of the complexity, discontinuity, and diversity that constitute race, ethnicity, and difference (Dervin, 1991; Fry, 1998; Olmsted, 1998; Rodriguez, 2003; Said, 2000).

In what follows I push forward this emergent transitive verb trend by viewing human beings as culturing beings. I define *culturing* as our proclivity to construct new and different meanings, understandings, and practices so as to reckon with the world's infinite ambiguity and quantum nature that constantly destabilize extant meanings, understandings, and practices. We are always constructing new and different ways of being and understanding the world, which is to say that cultures are always reckoning with instability and change. No culture is inherently stable and homogenous. Culturing is born out of our uniquely human need to bring meaning to bear upon the world's ambiguity. It represents the various tensions and rhythms that come with our trying to find and hold onto meanings in a world that is inherently quantum in consciousness. Thus, this paper forwards a quantum understanding of culture. Such an understanding, I argue, allows us to look anew at what being human means and expands moral action by locating our humanity within a potentially moral world. It answers the call for "a way to acknowledge and accept those aspects of dialectical inquiry that contribute to self-reflection and the appreciation of Otherness, and at the same time cultivate an awareness of those aspects that perpetuate symbolic violence" (McPhail, 1996, p. 150). It also gives us a theoretical and political way "to step back from the imaginary thresholds that separate people from each other" by releasing us from the dichotomous labels and positionalities that come with such thresholds (Said, 2001).

I begin with a look at the ontological foundation that makes cultures inherently quantum. Cultures are constantly negotiating the interplay between ambiguity and meaning, chaos and order, homogeneity and diversity, equilibrium and disequilibrium, agency and structure, and other such quantum and dialectical tensions. The result being that cultures are always in flux (Martin & Nakayama, 1999). I argue that cultures evolve and expand by encouraging the rich interplay between all quantum tensions, especially that of meaning and ambiguity (Bateson, 1994; Bohm, 1996). Through this evolution and expansion cultures promote the evolution of new and different ways of understanding and experiencing the world. What emerges is a culturing ethos that promotes interpretation and reinterpretation, and, in so doing, pushes us to be more open to new and different ways of understanding and experiencing the world. Such an ethos therefore blocks the formation of rigid positionalities that tend to pit us violently against each other (Bateson, 1994; Bohm, 1996; Said, 2000). I end with a discussion of three epistemological implications that a quantum understanding of culture brings to bear on intercultural communication theory.

The Relation Between Ambiguity and Meaning

Cultures are organic systems. As with other such systems, all cultures have points of homogeneity and diversity, continuity and discontinuity, stability and instability, meaning and ambiguity, order and chaos (Bohm, 1980; Capra, 1983; Gribbin, 1984; Herbert, 1987; Jantsch, 1980). Instinctively, cultures—like any other organic system—strive to affirm life so as to evolve and expand. Conversely, practices and forces that undercut the evolution of cultures make for the demise of such cultures. To survive and prosper cultures therefore have to change and evolve by promoting the forces and practices that make for change and evolution. Integral to the promotion of such change and evolution is ambiguity (Prigogine & Stengers, 1984).

Meaning and ambiguity are ontologically intertwined (Janstch, 1980; Prigogine & Stengers, 1984). A world devoid of ambiguity is one devoid of meaning. Each defines the other by making for the existence of each other. As such, ambiguity and meaning more than simply define each other; they actually constitute and embed each other. So there is always meaning in ambiguity and ambiguity in meaning. No meaning is ever completely stable, that is, ever beyond the reach of a new and different interpretation. There is much heuristic purchase in this inextricable relation between ambiguity and meaning. Ambiguity challenges us to look at the world anew. It expands our humanity by forcing us to develop new meanings, new ways of experiencing and being in the world. In this way, ambiguity fosters diversity and evolution. It is a life catalyst, or, according to Mary Catherine Bateson (1994), "the warp of life." Systems that focus deterministically on eliminating ambiguity allow for no growth, no evolution, and, ironically, no order (Bohm, 1996). Ambiguity therefore makes for open and vibrant systems—the only systems that evolve and strive.

Ambiguity makes for new experiences, new understandings, new ways of being, and new kinds of relations with each other by keeping meaning incomplete. Regardless of our most strenuous efforts, no meaning, again, is ever absolute, ever devoid of ambiguity, or ever devoid of interpretation. The ambiguity of the world keeps meaning in a constant state of flux and openness (Bateson, 1994). There is always the occasion for a new and different interpretation. Meaning is always multivocal and incomplete

(Bohm, 1996; Lee, Wang, et al. 1995). As such, ambiguity poses a constant threat to the status quo. It constantly pushes us to look at the world differently by inherently destabilizing how we understand the world. Yet it is this jamming that life finds inspiration through the realization of new interpretations. The inherent incomplete nature of meaning therefore makes our worlds and cultures quantum by constantly promoting the evolution of new ways of being and understanding the world. In worlds and cultures where meaning is embraced as being inherently incomplete, life evolves and prospers through the constant evolution of new and different meanings. Abdulkarim Soroush, who is seen by many scholars as Iran's boldest contemporary theologian, and who faces constant persecution from Iran's religious autocracy, makes this point well:

> The essence of religion will always be sacred, but its interpretation by fallible human beings is not sacred—and therefore can be criticized, modified, refined, and redefined. What single person can say what God meant? Any fixed version would effectively smother religion. It would block the rich exploration of the sacred texts. Interpretations are also influenced by the age you live in, by the conditions and mores of the era, and by other branches of that knowledge. So there's no single, inflexible, or absolute interpretation of Islam for all time. (Wright, 1999, pp. 46-47)

We can never end or completely command the world's ambiguity. It exceeds and precedes us. Yet without ambiguity life has no meaning. It is ambiguity that catalyzes and inspires our proclivity for meaning, and through meaning life finds expression and articulation. Still we persist in trying to rid the world of ambiguity. We claim that soon we will be able "to know the mind of God" and find the "final theory" that will explain the origins and workings of the world. Of course absolutism abounds many spheres of many cultures.

However, our ambition to end the world's ambiguity is born out of a deep fear of the world. We assume no moral, existential, or spiritual connection between the world and us. Instead, we assume that the world is in conflict with us and, consequently, our own survival and prosperity is dependent on us forcefully and coercively subduing and controlling the supposed malevolent forces of the world that seem bent on destroying us. We also assume that ambiguity threatens meaning. We focus on reducing and managing ambiguity. We construe the relation between meaning and ambiguity dualistically and oppositionally rather than dialectically and holistically. We remain committed to developing sciences, machines, and techniques that end the world's ambiguity, complexity, and mystery (Bohm, 1996).

But the world no longer seems tolerant of our ambitions to end its ambiguity. It seems to have had enough of the horrors that such an ambition exacts on the weak and innocent. So as we persist in the illusion of positing absolute and complete meanings, understandings, and truths, the world also seems to be reasserting its ambiguity, complexity, and diversity. For example, we are increasingly dismantling long held notions of race, ethnicity, sexuality, and religion. More and more of us belong to every place, every race, and worship all Gods. We are more and more writing about racing, placing, and hopefully soon, culturing. Understandings of identity are becoming increasingly complex, incomplete, and fluid (Chen & Starosta, 1996). We are increasingly describing ourselves as human rather than, say, Antiguan or Indian; sexual rather than heterosexual or homosexual; spiritual rather than religious, and so forth. New sciences, writings, paradigms, and fields of study that stress union rather than separation are also emerging. And though Nobel Laureate Steven Weinberg promises to uphold reductionism to the end, holism is seen by other Nobel

Laureates like Freeman Dyson and Ilya Prigogine as the path we must now take to understand a world that ontologically resists absolute and complete truths and understandings (see Weinberg, 1995 & 2001). Ambiguity, again, will always exceed and precede meaning.

Communication is also acknowledging this emergent quantum worldview and reflecting different ways that it reshapes and expands our understanding of communication (Contractor, 1994; Cottone, 1993; McPhail, 1996; Murphy, 1996; Seeger, Sellnow, & Ulmer, 1998; Witte, Meyer, et al., 1996). McPhail (1996) contends that this emergent paradigm makes for a new rhetoric by getting us beyond the separation that duality fosters. Our "belief in separatedness has, indeed, made us strangers, and has created a language of negative difference which manifests itself in the social and symbolic spaces of race, gender, and rhetoric" (p 66).

I look next at how a quantum understanding of the relation between ambiguity and meaning helps us identify communication practices that promote the evolution of cultures and, thereby, more constructive ways of negotiating our infinite differences. I examine the potentiality of such an understanding to help "lessen the threats of our differences" by drawing upon the intertwine relation between homogeneity and diversity.

Rhythms, Tensions, and Meanings

All organic systems have points of disequilibrium that constantly disrupt the status quo. These points reflect different interpretations, meanings, and truths that make for conflict and dissent. For example, forests fires resulting from natural forces represent points of disequilibrium. Yet such fires are vital for the well-being of forests by allowing for the burning of underbrush and old trees that encumber forests' ecosystems from evolving and flourishing. Points of disequilibrium perform a vital function by blocking natural systems from becoming completely homogeneous, that is, from becoming beholden to one understanding of the world. Moreover, such points undercut the reifying and deifying of certain ways of being and, in so doing, act as catalysts for evolution and transformation. Conversely, through the suppression of such points organic systems lose the ability to respond flexibly and creatively to new situations. Points of disequilibrium therefore affirm life by constantly contesting and disrupting the status quo; pushing the system to realize new expressions.

So all cultures possess a striving to evolve, and through such evolution find prosperity. But such evolution is dependent on cultures promoting the rich interplay between meaning and ambiguity. This requires cultures realizing those rhythms that promote new meanings and interpretations while simultaneously allowing for the devolution of current meanings and interpretations. Integral to finding these rhythms is the promotion of ways of being that encourage the incomplete nature of meaning, that is, understandings of communication that promote interpretation rather than transmission. As McPhail observes (1996), "Communication, as it has been practiced and continues to be practiced in Western culture, is geared towards social control and the maintenance of existing ideological and epistemological structures" (p. 138). However, such an understanding of communication still pervades intercultural communication theory (Martin & Nakayama, 1999; McPhail, 1996). In many cases, we still treat communication as a medium phenomenon—communication conveys and articulates culture. Communication emerges as a representational rather than ontological phenomenon, which is to say a way of representing rather than a way of embodying our worlds. In persisting in looking at communication in terms of transmission, we help perpetuate the view that cultures are stable and homogenous and thus amenable to reductionistic methodologies that strive to make complete and absolute claims.

Viewing communication as transmission—a bedrock assumption of popular definitions of culture—assumes that human beings are passive to the world. We are supposedly molded by prevailing discursive, communicative, and performative practices. We conceptualize the relationship between culture and communication as causal and deterministic (Martin & Nakayama, 1999). We assume that cultural patterns can theoretically predict behavior. Accordingly, exaggerated notions of stability and homogeneity permeate many popular definitions of culture (Dervin, 1991; Martin & Nakayama, 1999; Moon, 1996). Deetz (1995) contends that viewing communication as transmission misses the politics of self construction. It depoliticizes communication by masking issues of identity formation and blocking scrutiny of the deep ideological structures that constrict meaning creation processes. For Deetz (1995), " Communication is about dialogic, collaborative constructions of self, other, and world in the process of making collective decisions. This includes the production and reproduction of personal identities, social knowledge, and social structures" (p. 107). Communication places and displaces us. It simultaneously gives us an understanding of the world while simultaneously undercutting that understanding of the world. For instance, we never mirror our experiences or our thoughts. Each retelling creates new experiences, new meanings, new understandings, and, often, even new truths. In this way, communication enables us by affording us constant access to new experiences, new meanings, and new understandings (Arthos, 2000; Gordon, 2000).

A quantum world needs understandings of communication that can speak to its quantum proclivity. Such understandings can be found in emergent definitions of communication that ontologically assume no separation between communication and the world (e.g., Bohm, 1996; Thayer, 1995). Such definitions stress a consequential rather than referential understanding of communication (Thayer, 1995). That is, emergent definitions of communication hold to the quantum notion that the world and us are embedded within each other. Communication situates us in the world rather than is the means to represent the world. As Thayer (1995) notes, "In naming the world, we name ourselves; in explaining the world, we explain ourselves; in defining the world, we define ourselves" (p. 9). Through communication we construct as well as embody our worlds. However, such constructing and embodying is by no means arbitrary. As Martin Buber, Paulo Freire, David Bohm, and many other proponents of dialogue long argued, some communication practices are more heuristic and humane than others. Those practices that embrace ambiguity pull us towards the center of the world and thereby align us with the world's quantum rhythms. Such communication practices allow us to ebb and flow to these tensions. Meaning remains open and fluid and, in being so, allows us to also remain open and fluid. Thus how we embody, construct, understand, and relate to the world are all deeply intertwine and inseparable processes.

But many practices threaten the rich interplay between ambiguity and meaning. Arguably, one of the most serious and insidious is that of reification. Reification is the gateway to alienation and deification. It aims to limit human action by limiting ambiguity. It seduces us by limiting the anxiety that comes with ambiguity. In limiting human action, however, reification limits volition and, consequently, responsibility. It thus limits our obligation and commitment to each other and, in so doing, promotes separation and fragmentation. Reification also encumbers the evolution of new and different ways of being and understanding the world by promoting rigidity rather than flexibility. It does so by subtly turning us away from the world's ambiguity. We thereby lose the courage to fully embrace the ambiguity that is vital for new thoughts, ideas, experiences, understandings, and meanings to enter the world. In this way, reification also undercuts diversity and plurality. Finally, reification blocks the formation of the deep and complex human relations that flow from vibrant meaning creation and interpretive processes. In *Developing Through Relationships*, Alan Fogel (1993) writes about how reification harms the evolution of such relations:

When relationships evolve into patterns in which participants perceive them as sequences of discrete exchanges or reward and cost it is quite likely that the creativity has gone out of them. They are no longer dynamic systems in which individuals grow, they have become prisons of the soul. Repeated encounters, therefore, can sometimes dull the senses and produce hatred, anger, and boredom. It is not mere repetition that leads to creative elaboration, it is one's stance toward the other, one's openness to change and desire to create new meaning through the relationship. (p. 90)

Fogel also writes that "Relationships must have . . . something not quite known, something that may never be understood or even articulated, something that entices the mind and body and that renews the meaning in the relationship" (p. 90). Put differently, cultures evolve by promoting incompletion. But more importantly, through the

Diversity

promotion of incompletion we also realize our own potentiality to construct realities that actually promote diversity and plurality. Incompletion therefore encourages a dialogic communication sensibility.

Such a sensibility assumes that we quest for completion, that we possess the capacity to act deliberately upon the world, that we become fully human only through practices that promote affirmation, empathy, openness, and trust, that an existential, moral, and even spiritual relation exists between the world and us, and that the world is incomplete (Arnett, 1986; Buber, 1970 & 1994; Cissna & Anderson, 1994; Freire, 1993; Gordon, 2000; Murray, 2000; Shotter, 2000). Through dialogic communication we contribute to the world's creation and completion. Our becoming is entwined with that of the world. Practices that harm our becoming also harm the becoming of the world. As such, a dialogic sensibility encourages us to be open, sensitive, and tolerant of new ways of understanding and experiencing the world (Czubaroff & Friedman, 2000; Pearce & Littlejohn, 1997). We are to dialogue with (rather than against) others to achieve mutual understandings and realize new possibilities.

I now look at three different ways that culturing expands intercultural communication theory and heightens the ferment emerging in intercultural communication studies that views culture relationally, dialectically, and holistically (Belay, 1993; Casmir, 1993; Martin & Nakayama, 1999; McPhail, 1996; Shuter, 1993; Starosta, 1991).

New Vistas and New Possibilities

Understandably, intercultural communication theory has a deep tradition against claims of different cultures being morally superior to other cultures. Much good has come from upholding this tradition. But emergent observations of the world are forcing us to reckon with the claim that we have no ontological or epistemological ground upon which to make moral claims about different cultures. To look at cultures from a quantum standpoint allows us to move beyond the horrors that attend to cultural hegemony while simultaneously allowing us to make moral claims about different cultures. We accomplish this feat in the most interesting of ways.

Adopting a culturing standpoint reveals how the constant evolving and changing nature of cultures constantly undermines efforts to establish and sustain cultural hegemony. Culturing highlights the quantum tensions and contradictions that define all cultures. We simultaneously see the homogeneity and diversity, the stability and instability, the order and the chaos, and so forth. We also see the political, moral, and existential struggles, and the many contests over meanings, interpretations, and symbols that define all cultures. We ultimately come to understand that claims of cultural uniformity and stability will always be illusory. There will always be spaces where hope resides.

Thus culturing gives us a moral direction rather than a moral destination. It promotes communication practices that stress diversity, sensitivity, and other ways of being that make or intend for no harm to others and the world. In this way, culturing does make for a superior morality. For example, cultures where peoples of different understandings, truths, and even gods, live peacefully with each other are indeed morally superior to other cultures where such peoples are persecuted, maimed, and killed for simply being Other. In sum, culturing does give us a way to understand which communication and cultural practices acknowledge and appreciate Otherness and difference, while at the same time cultivating "an awareness of those aspects that perpetuate symbolic violence" (McPhail, 1996, p. 150).

But culturing gives us more than a moral direction. It also acknowledges, even celebrates, the cultural commonalities that morally bound us together, and, in so doing, "lessens the threats of our [cultural] differences." All cultures are constantly grappling with the interplay between ambiguity and meaning and the other quantum tensions that this interplay sets off. Yet culturing demystifies cultures without destroying or infringing on their inherent complexity. It gives us a heuristic means to understand cultures without making us believe that our understandings can ever be or need to be complete and absolute. Cultural complexity makes for inherent mystery. But now we no longer need to be afraid of this mystery. It reflects the infinite potentiality that undergirds all cultures. So whereas intercultural communication theory has long focused on describing what is, culturing allows us now to also consider what can be and also what needs to be.

Finally, in a world where recent horrendous events seem to be endorsing the hypothesis about the coming "clash of civilizations," culturing reframes our understanding of cultures in a way that neither undermines hope nor the possibility of us forging new ways of being together with others who seem to be so culturally different and alien to us, even to the point of being seen as less human than us. Hope resides in the points of disruption, disequilibrium, and dissent that constantly destabilize the status quo. Hope also resides in the quantum tugging found in all organic systems. No culture can escape the quantum order of the world. Cultures that focus on ending ambiguity and diversity will eventually devolve. The quantum order of the world will tolerate only so much variability. In this way, though never certain, redemption is always possible; that is, there is always the possibility for more constructive and nonviolent ways of being together to emerge and make for new realities. Thus "for future generations to condemn themselves to prolonged war and suffering without so much as a critical pause, without looking at interdependent histories of injustice and oppression, without trying for common emancipation and mutual understanding seems far more willful than necessary" (Said, 2001).

Final Thoughts

Verbing our understanding of culture assumes that human beings are fundamentally relational beings with a striving and potentiality for communion with the world and each other. We are culturing beings—always constructing and deconstructing cultures. Common understandings of culture mask the natural tensions that cultures possess and which are so vital for their prosperity. This, again, is a world of chaos and order, ambiguity and meaning, homogeneity and diversity, stability and instability, and equilibrium and disequilibrium. Cultures, like all organic entities, are constantly negotiating these quantum tensions. Yet these tensions are natural catalysts for life's evolution and expansion. Through the evolution and expansion of our cultures our humanity evolves and expands. It seems therefore that our redemption and that of the world is sacredly intertwined.

II
Spanglish And The Quest For Possibility

In a quantum world, that is, one laden with tensions, nothing can ever remain pure and stable. Rhythm is status quo. It is what reminds us that the world demands evolution from us. We could, of course, decide to resist and obstruct the world's passion for evolution, but such actions would only make for our demise. So let the world have its rhythms of disruption and evolution. These are the rhythms of redemption—the ones that promise to reveal the world's beauty and potentiality. In my view, these rhythms are most compellingly seen in the rise of Spanglish.

We are now bending and stretching identity in ways that are unparallel in human history. "Movement is [indeed] status quo," and the movement that Ed Morales (2002) is referring to in *Living in Spanglish: The Search for Latino Identity in America* is what many Latinos throughout the U.S. are fondly calling Spanglish.

At the root of Spanglish is a very universal state of being. It is a displacement from one place, home, to another place, home, in which one feels at home in both places, yet at home in neither place. It is a kind of banging-one's-head-against-the-wall state, and the only choice you have left is to embrace the transitory (read transnational) state of in-between. (Morales, 2002, p. 7)

Spanglish is a "forward-looking race that obliterates all races" by embracing all races. In other words, it is "a call to end race" as we commonly understand race. "But in order to face down race, we must first immerse ourselves in it. In all of them" (Morales, 2002, p. 14). Moreover, Spanglish is "a space where multiple levels of identification is possible" (Morales, 2002, p. 17), akin, Morales believes, to what Michel Foucault calls a heterotopic space—"a kind of effectively enacted utopia in which all the other real sites that can be found within the culture are simultaneously represented, contested, and inverted" (quoted in Morales, 2002, p. 17). Spanglish is also akin to what Pico Iyer (2000) describes in *The Global Soul: Jet lag, Shopping Malls, and the Search for Home* as the global soul—a person who "has grown up in many cultures all at once—and so lived in the cracks between them" (p. 18).

Spanglish is therefore more than a long-term racial miscegenation process occurring among Latinos in the U.S., and definitely more than the evolution of a language that fuses English and Spanish. It is, in fact, about the evolution of an identity that is finally disconnected—liberated, really—from one race, one place, one space, one language, one vision, one history, and so on. As such, "there is no prescribed form, no cultural norms involved in being Spanglish—the world of Spanglish is the world of the multiracial individual" (Morales, 2002, p. 9). It is the culture of the future because it has no score to settle with the past. More importantly, Spanglish is simply—and finally—about more and more persons recognizing that the future will always afford more possibilities than the past. It represents the triumph of heterogeneity, multisubjectivity, and multiplicity, and celebrates a "permanently evolving, and rapidly expanding difference" (Morales, 2002, p. 26). In this way, Spanglish is about the end of culture—and race and ethnicity—as a noun.

It is about culturing. In other words, Spanglish demonstrates that no culture, no race, no ethnicity, no language, is inherently stable and homogenous.

A world laden with weapons of mass destruction can no longer afford conflict and strife between peoples that construct identity through a purely physical conception of space. Thus in disconnecting identity from space, Spanglish finally allows us to imagine a world devoid of such conflict and strife. In releasing identity from space, Spanglish allows us to imagine more expansive and inclusive models of identity, and, thereby, more expansive and inclusive models of space. As such, releasing identity from geography in no way weakens identity. Identity, as with other any other organic system, too must change and evolve to survive and prosper, and such change is only possible when our models of identity remain fluid and permeable. This is exactly what Spanglish is about. It represents the fullest expression of identity in terms of social evolution.

Spanglish is also increasingly making us global souls. It frees us from the rigid confines of one race, one ethnicity, one language, one geography, one people, one culture, one history, one reality, one worldview, one god. Such confines only serve to distort and limit what we can become. The evolution of Spanglish also signals that increasing numbers of us are refusing to be confined to one race, one ethnicity, one culture, one geography, and no one probably understood this better than Eddie Figueroa, a New York conceptual artist, who Ed Morales discusses in *Living in Spanglish*.

Morales (2002) writes that Figueroa was thoroughly obsessed with Latinos being a "multicultural people and that there was no space for us in the conventional world, and we had to invent an imaginary space to allow us to gel" (p. 90). He believed this space could be found in the concept of the

Puerto Rican Embassy, which evolved later into the Spirit Republic of Greater Puerto Rico. According to Figueroa,

> The Puerto Rican Embassy is a concept, it's an idea, it's not a physical location. . . . We are dealing with concepts that are beyond geography, beyond three dimensions. With the Puerto Rican Embassy, we're declaring our independence. The spirit republic is a free place. To win this fight we don't need weapons, this is the weapon that's going to win [points to heart]. The revolution is here, man. (quoted in Morales, 2002, p. 91).

As Morales (2002) acknowledges, Figueroa did indeed make "it a little easier for Puerto Ricans to be several people at once, in several places, looking backward from the future into the past . . . . It is an idea that is no longer as bizarre as it seemed" (p. 92).

Check Miscellaneous

In *The Global Soul*, Pico Iyer (2000) wonders about whether there is a migratory striving that is making us global souls. He quotes Simone Weil ("We must take the feeling of being at home into exile. We must be rooted in the absence of place."), Thomas Paine ("My country is the world, and my religion is to do good."), and Ralph Waldo Emerson ("What is man but a congress of nations?"). He seems uncertain as to what to make exactly of this global soul phenomenon. On one hand, Iyer (2000) believes that "our shrinking world gave more and more of us the chance to see, in palpable, unanswerable ways, how much we [have] in common, and how much we could live . . . beyond petty allegiances and labels, out-side the reach of nation-states"

(p. 17). He also writes, "I have grown up, too, with a keen sense of the blessings of being unaffiliated, it has meant that almost everywhere is new and strange to me (as I am new and strange to it), and nearly everywhere allows me to keep alive a sense of wonder and detachment" (Iyer, 2000, p. 24). On the other hand, Iyer (2000) fears that "A lack of affiliation may mean a lack of accountability, and forming a sense of commitment can be hard without a sense of community" (p. 25). Moreover, "Displacement can encourage the wrong kinds of distance, and if the nationalism we see sparking up around the globe arises from too narrow and fixed sense of loyalty, the internationalism that's coming to birth may reflect too roaming and undefined sense of belonging" (Iyer, 2000, p. 25). Further, "The Global Soul may see so many sides of every question that he never settles on a firm conviction; he may grow so used to giving back a different self according to his environment that he loses sight of who he is when nobody's around" (Iyer, 2000, p. 25). Yet Iyer (2000) uses the phrase global soul, never global citizen, global people, nor even global being. He never explains why he uses the word soul, but I believe it speaks to how he experiences his own being in the world, his own evolution from the primal to the spiritual. This is the phrase I would have used. No other phrase better captures my own transcending of race, ethnicity, nationality, and geography.

I too am a global soul. I too am Spanglish. I too am Brown. I too am a Nowherian. I too live between home and exile. I too feel like a congress of nations dwells within me. I too struggle to break free from the confines of one race, one gender, one sexuality, one nationality, one ethnicity, one geography. I too am against the tyranny of borders. I too feel like the half-English, half-Japanese, Malaysian man who says to Iyer, "One country is not enough" (quoted in Iyer, 2000, p. 18). But I would also add "One race is not enough."

Diversity

"One ethnicity is not enough." "One culture is not enough." "One cosmology is not enough." "One religion is not enough." "One language is not enough." "One sexuality is not enough."

We feel surrounded, that's the thing. Our borders do not hold. National borders do not hold. Ethnic borders. Religious borders. Aesthetics borders, certainly. Sexual borders. Allergenic borders. We live in the "Age of diversity," in a city of diversity—I do, anyway—so we see what we do not necessarily choose to see: People listing according to internal weathers. We hear what we do not want to hear: Confessions we refuse to absolve. (p. 213)
Brown: The Last Discovery of America
Richard Rodríguez

Iyer wonders whether we have a migratory impulse. We have, after all, always been moving from place to place. We have never remained confined to one place or space. Movement is status quo. Iyer, however, under-appreciates the movement that is occurring. It is in no way purely migratory. It is much more than people having multiple passports, living in airports, and travelling all over the planet like desperate cultural, racial, and ethnic nomads. In my view, the global soul, as in Spanglish, represents the highest evolutionary point so far in human history. In fact, the global soul represents the end of history and the coming of a new world—one that ends long held beliefs, values, truths, and norms. Nothing will no longer be the same.

Inevitably, the question will arise from someone: "Who am I?" which translates to really mean "Where are you originally from?" "What is your race?" "Which box do you check off?" "What exactly is your ethnicity?" "What is your first language?" "Did I pronounce your name correctly?" "Where is your accent from?" "Do you miss home?" I never want to answer any of these questions. After all, Why does it matter where I am from? Or what is my race or ethnicity? But I in no way want to suggest that I am one of those persons who is simply trying to be raceless and spaceless so as to avoid the hassles and responsibilities that come with race and ethnicity. I embrace race and own the history of all races. In wanting to avoid answering these questions I am identifying with all of the world's oppressed peoples, regardless of race, ethnicity, gender, religion, sexual orientation, or nationality. Still, I believe that answering these questions help perpetuate a hegemony and world order that I wish to help destroy—the very one that attempts to disconnect my well-being from the poverty stricken people in some ghetto in, say, Brazil. Moreover, these questions have nothing to do with what I am about and the life that I am desperately trying to embody. I really do want to undermine the social ordering and control that commonly-held notions of identity help to perpetuate. But I have grown into this politics.

There were never any boxes for me. There was always one problem or the other. Friends would fondly advise I check the box "Miscellaneous." Of course miscellaneous really means illegitimate. In many ways this is what I am and I what I wish to be. I want to be illegitimate. I want never to be easily categorized, for to be categorized is to say this is what I am, and this subtly bounds me to the present. I wish to belong to the future. I want my illegitimacy to disrupt the dominant order, to push us to ask questions we never once thought of asking, to challenge us to explore realities that seem impossible, and to invite us to imagine worlds that seem unimaginable. So when I am categorized by others as Miscellaneous, or must simply check the box marked Other, as big as the box probably is, I have to resist because to do otherwise is to facilitate my own marginalization and help sustain the legitimacy of a network of power relations that is only harming the world. In other words, in refusing to be boxed, I am saying that this world is laden with the potential for other realities and possibilities, and many of these realities and possibilities may never lend for any category. I am also saying that the no institution has any moral authority to sort us like fruits and vegetables.

But what exactly about the boxes given to us as norm that are so legitimate? What about even the need to box people like fruit and vegetables? The congress of nations that dwells within me will never allow me to be easily boxed. This is one way I understand Spanglish. It represents the rise of Miscellaneous and the end of categorization. It is about a way of being that defies the concepts and precepts that sustain the status quo. It is about the end of exclusion and separation and the rise of our own evolutionary impulse to defy the forces and practices that impede our social evolution and liberation. So I believe that our impulse to move from one space to the next is really an evolutionary striving, and practices that impede this striving ultimately undermine our prosperity and survival. Thus unlike Iyer, I have no doubts or suspicions about the coming of the global soul. In fact, I look forward to its coming.

Spanglish and the Critics

But I have no illusions about the coming of the global soul and the rise of Spanglish. I know the status quo really wants global consumers rather than global souls. I have fears about Spanglish being reduced to merely a language. I also fear this language acquiring all the trappings of a language of power—one that terrorizes those who lack a command of the language. I also know that evolution and destruction are dialectically intertwined, and, for this reason, evolution causes us much anxiety. I therefore understand the harsh criticisms Spanglish is catching from Latinos, especially from the Latino intelligentsia. For example, Nobel Laureate Octavio Paz describes Spanglish as an abomination ("Ni es bueno ni es malo, sino abominable.") (quoted in Stavans, 2000a, p. 555). Moreover, besides finding Spanglish offensive, Roberto González Echevarría (1997), Sterling Professor of Hispanic and Comparative Literature at Yale University, believes that "it is naïve to think that we [U.S. Latinos] could create a new language that would functional and culturally rich" as Spanish. He believes that Spanglish "poses a grave danger to Hispanic culture and to the advancement of Hispanics in mainstream America" (Gonzalez Echevarría, 1997, p. A.29). "Spanglish is an invasion of Spanish by English" (Gonzalez Echevarría, 1997, p. A.29). Gonzalez Echevarría (1997) also believes "that people should learn languages well and that learning English should be the priority for Hispanics, if they aspire, as they should, to influential positions" (p. A.29). Those who practice Spanglish "are doomed to writing not a minority literature but a minor literature." Indeed, Gonzalez Echevarría makes no apologies for believing that "Spanish is our strongest bond, and it is vital that we preserve it" (p. A.29). Likewise, Antonio Garrido, director of the Instituto Cervantes in New York, an organization created by the Spanish government to promote Spanish and Hispanic-American language and culture, believes that Latinos should strive for good English and good Spanish so as "to have a future" in the United States. "Spanglish has no future" (quoted in Kong, 2003). For Claudio Véliz (1994):

There is irony in the choice of this ghastly but accurate descriptive name for what passes for Spanish in many . . .

regions. "Spanglish" is, pseudonationalistic protestations notwithstanding, an unseemly, scarcely literate linguistic hodgepodge that would not be tolerated in any country within hearing distance of the Real Academia. The irony is that the admixture of extraneous bits of flotsam, the adulteration of spelling and syntaxes, and the virtual abandonment of all grammatical decorum are only possible because this patois found shelter in the ambit of the Gothic fox. Every time they open their mouths, the users of "Spanglish" proclaim *urbi et orbi* that they have embraced the "mental habits," the cultural dispositions, and the customs of the English-speaking host nation with enthusiasm, and to prove it, they present their listeners with the tattered, pitiful remains of the language they inherited from Nebrija. (p. 125)

I understand why Spanglish's critics have such deep anxieties. The nature of the criticisms should in no way surprise us. We have seen these criticisms again and again. Just recently, in fact, we saw Ebonics take the same kind of beating from the African American intelligentsia. In defense of Spanglish, Illan Stavans (2000b) recounts, for example, that Yiddish was never a unified tongue, but rather a series of regional varieties drawn from Hebrew, German, Russian, and other Slavic languages. In fact, such was the contempt for Yiddish that rabbis and the Jewish intelligentsia saw Yiddish as unworthy of biblical dialogue. In 1978, however, the Yiddish author Isaac Bashevis Singer was awarded the Nobel Prize in Literature.

Nativists who want to declare English the official language of the United States do not understand the omnivorous appetite of the language they wish to protect. Neither do they understand that their protection would harm our tongue. . . . Those Americans who would build a fence around American English to forestall the Trojan burrito would turn American into a frightened tongue, a shrinking

little oyster tongue, as French has lately become, priested over by the Ancients of the Academie, who fret so about le weekend. (p. 112)
 Brown: The Last Discovery of America
 Richard Rodríguez

Spanglish's critics view Spanglish as a dirty dialect that threatens to pollute Spanish and English. This is always the first salvo. If Spanglish has no legitimacy, it has no authenticity. We now have permission to abuse and destroy it. This criticism appeals viscerally to us because of our own distrust and suspicion of the human condition. Spanglish emerges as a debased language form—a product of backward and primitive peoples. This is why its critics believe that it has no ability to produce great literature and why they harp on social class issues. For instance, Gonzalez Echevarría (1997) says, "The sad reality is that Spanglish is primarily the language of poor Hispanics, many barely literate in either language. They incorporate English words and constructions into their daily speech because they lack the vocabulary and education in Spanish to adapt to the changing culture around them" (p. A.29). He also fears that various groups would carve out their own Spanglish, "creating a Babel of hybrid tongues" (p. A.29). But the story of Babel has nothing to do with language. Language is merely an artifact of communication. It is by no means the sum of communication or even the primary constitution of communication. That honor belongs to compassion. With compassion, understanding is always possible. As such, the story of Babel is really about the social problems that come with the lack of compassion.

But when was language ever pure? Linguistic purity, as even Gonzalez Echevarría (1997) acknowledges, is an illusion. It is an ideological artifact. Languages are inherently promiscuous—a promiscuity that reflects us bending and twisting and recreating language to speak to new and different experiences and influences. This is why, for instance, Spanish can be so different from one place to the next. Linguistic impurity speaks to the ever evolving and changing nature of language to be inclusive rather than exclusive. As long as human beings use language, linguistic impurity will be the order of language. To attempt to keep any language pure is simply to promote the demise of that language. But more than that, language purity is really about clinging to racial purity and ideological stability. It is about the promotion of exclusion and the preservation of the status quo. Thus in linguistic impurity we find ethnic and racial impurity. We find our impulse to move beyond the separation and fragmentation that ethnic and racial purity promotes and perpetuates. We can always settle for bilingualism. But bilingualism is merely about access to different spaces. Spanglish takes us much further. It represents the mutual joining and sharing of spaces and places. As Morales (2002) notes, "The mixing of language that occurs in Spanglish is a metaphor for the mixture of race; it allows for races to have different voices in the same language, eliminating the need to structure language, or thinking in terms of racial category" (p. 48).

Spanglish shows us linguistically, communicatively, and epistemologically forging the means to find harmony in this world. This is why Spanglish is emerging and blossoming in the most heterogeneous spaces and places in the world, like New York and Los Angeles. This is also why Spanglish is emerging from the bottom social and economic classes—those persons who lack the economic means to spatially avoid other peoples by moving out to affluent hyper-suburbs and gated-communities. Exclusion is an option only for those persons who are economically privileged. But exclusion is also death. Inclusion is the order of organic systems. It represents interconnectedness and embeddedness. It also represents the end of isolation and rejection. Spanglish is about the rise of inclusion in a world where exclusion, unfortunately, is status quo. Its blatant and bold inclusion of two distinct languages speak to an inclusion that wants nothing to do with the assimilation that so many persons who craft national policy believe is the only way to deal with an increasingly diverse U.S. society. In fact, Spanglish moves us boldly beyond the assimilation/toleration divide. We no longer have to claim, as even many prominent defenders of toleration do, that one is merely the lesser of two evils. That is, we no longer have to make believe that an increasingly diverse society requires morally awkward and imperfect frameworks to maintain peace and prosperity.

Spanglish reminds us that inclusion has always been the order of the world. We have always been interconnected. Buddhists, Hindus, and Jains have been teaching this reality for hundred of years. The separation we cling to is illusory, and will always be illusory. Our quest for exclusion, either racially, linguistically, ethnically, and spatially, is therefore also illusory. We will always be interconnected. The issue is one of degree: *How interconnected and embedded are we willing to be? How steadfast are we going to remain to promoting and reifying the illusion of separation and fragmentation? How much of a price are we willing to pay to sustain to this illusion?*

In the end, Ed Morales's *Spanglish* makes for much more compelling reading than Richard Rodriguez's *Brown*. Rodriguez (2002) believes that our redemption resides in the brown peoples that miscegenation produces. Through the rise of this brown race we will ultimately end the various racisms that have long bedevilled us. Rodriguez (2002) has no interest in interrogating the deep ideological apparatuses that promote separation, exclusion, and inequality. He is fixated with race. He also has no interest in either cosmology or ontology. Ed Morales, on the other hand, is all about cosmology and ontology. This is why he uniquely recognizes that Spanglish is more than a language. Even Illan Stavans (2000b), who is cited in nearly every media report about Spanglish as the leading authority on the subject, treats Spanglish as merely a language that deserves a semblance of acceptance. In locating Spanglish at the level of ontology—"Living in Spanglish"—Morales shows an ambition to disrupt the status quo. Rodriguez (2002) has no such ambition. He wants recognition and appreciation of the browning of the U.S. Other than that, Rodriguez has no issue with the U.S. In fact, Rodriguez adores Richard Nixon.

No doubt, the U.S. is browning and this change will significantly impact U.S. society. But to reduce this browning to purely a racial phenomenon is to downplay what this browning is and what the rise of brown really means for the U.S. Brown is the color of creation. The rise of brown is evolutionary. It represents the end of old biases, prejudices, and suspicions. Brown is meant to disrupt the status quo, and, no doubt, Richard Rodriguez (2002) would contend that this is happening. But Rodriguez (2002) is under-appreciating what is happening. We are more than browning racially. We are also browning cosmologically, ontologically, epistemologically, existentially, and ideologically. Spanglish captures this browning. Spanglish is brown, very brown as a matter of fact. Rodriguez (2002) would have us believe that Brown represents an organic model of assimilation. But Brown wants nothing to do with assimilation. There is no fecundity in assimilation. No possibility for revolution. No possibility for liberation. Rodriguez (2002) makes Brown palatable and fashionable. He does so by depoliticizing and defanging Brown. In other words, Rodriguez (2002) ideologically hollows out Brown. For Rodriguez (2002), I simply represent the rise of a new race. He has no interest in my politics, that is, no concern for the forces that animate my being. Morales, however, has a fuller and better appreciation of my being. He understands and embraces the threat my brown poses to the status quo.

We will increasingly have to choose between Richard Rodriguez's brown and Ed Morales' brown. I, of course, choose the latter. I do so because inclusion is about entering the world with all of our being, and I own the fact that I am brown in my soul, in my language, in my pedagogy, and in my politics. I choose Morales' brown because I am willing to bear the burden this brown places on me.

Final Thoughts

Linguistic diversity and equality are no doubt vital to attaining and preserving human dignity and peace in the world. However, as Lee Chong-Yeong (2003) points out, "Linguistic politics is increasingly becoming a destabilizing factor of world peace and justice" (p. 58). He blames "linguistic hegemonism and linguistic egoism" for causing conflicts throughout the world and for promoting linguistic incommunicability, linguistic injustice, and linguistic injustice, all of which undermine justice and world peace. The solution to all of these problems, according to Chong-Yeong (2003), lies in the promotion of an ethnically neutral auxiliary language, such as Esperanto.

But Chong-Yeong, as with many other political scientists, makes a major theoretical error in analysis. Linguistic hegemonism and linguistic egoism are merely expressions and symptoms of larger forces that torment linguistic diversity and equality, and, by that, world peace and justice. In other words, linguistic hegemonism and linguistic egoism are artifacts of cosmological and ideological hegemonism, egoism, and chauvinism. The problem therefore has to be attacked at the cosmological and ideological level, and I would contend that doing so involves focusing beyond changing the sounds and symbols that come out of our mouths, but actually changing our relation to language and how we embody language. That is, an increasingly multicultural world demands of us a new language paradigm, and this paradigm is compelling seen in Spanglish.

To truly achieve world peace and justice require we disrupt the cosmological and ideological systems that seek world domination by pushing the theoretical flawed belief that linguistic purity, linguistic homogeneity, and linguistic stability are vital to attaining civility and progress. As long as this belief remains intact and hegemonic, linguistic diversity and equality will forever remain in peril, and thereby any possibility for world peace and justice will always elude us. As such, Spanglish gives us a new language model, as well as a new way of framing linguistic politics. Our goal, of course, should in no way be to encourage the world to adopt Spanglish. After all, left to its own organic devices and impulses, Spanglish will inherently subvert this colonization, regardless of how benevolent our intention. Instead, our goal should be to use Spanglish as a model to show other peoples throughout the world the promise of a new language model that can genuinely help attain peace and prosperity without sacrificing linguistic diversity and equality.

III
The Challenge of The New Mestizas

Samuel Huntington is once again blaming those of us who are of different worlds, and who move between worlds, and who claim to be citizens of the world, for all that is wrong with the world. In *Clash of Civilizations and the Remaking of World Order*, a book published in 1995 and subsequently translated into over 33 languages, Huntington warned of a coming Armageddon between the West and other civilizations. He said that the West needed to prepare itself for this coming clash by rejecting multiculturalism, bilingualism, and other threats to its ideological stability. After September 11, Huntington and the phrase clash of civilizations were everywhere. Now, in *Who We Are: The Challenges to America's National Identity*, Huntington (2004) focuses on the US and the threats that multiculturalism, bilingualism, postmodernism, postcolonialism, cosmopolitanism, globalism, and, especially, Latino immigration pose to the US.

He believes that these threats constitute the greatest challenge to our "existing cultural, political, legal, commercial, and educational systems," and "to the historical, cultural, and linguistic identity" of the US. He even contends that Latino immigration threatens the territorial integrity of the US. He calls for immediate and drastic actions to neutralize all of these threats.

Diversity 45

Such ominous warnings are in no way new. Ever since the dawn of history, one group of human beings has warned about the dire threat that a next group of human beings poses to their well-being. It is probably the oldest of human dramas. Yet it is also the most violent of human dramas. For every instance of ethnic cleansing is about this drama. Huntington is therefore merely giving voice and legitimacy to anxieties and suspicions that most of us already harbor. Still, what makes Huntington significant for analysis is that he has the academic privilege in being Chairman of the Harvard Academy for International and Area Studies and also The Albert J. Weatherhead III University Professor at Harvard University, titles and affiliation which are always noted by the media as a sign of great prophetic authority, to unfairly heighten these anxieties and insecurities. Thus reviews of *Who We Are* begin with sentences like, "Samuel Huntington is one of the most eminent political scientist in the world" (New York Times), "Samuel Huntington is a distinguished scholar who always addresses important and timely issues" (Los Angeles Times), "In the course of a remarkable distinguished academic career, Samuel Huntington has demonstrated a steadfast commitment to realism" (Foreign Policy Journal), "Harvard scholar Samuel Huntington [is] the most important political scientist in America. His last book, *The Clash of Civilizations*, forecasted the civilizational tensions that became obvious to everyone in the post-9/11 world. When Huntington writes, people listen—or they should" (National Review), "Samuel Huntington, of Harvard University, has a knack for giving sharp voice to issues which have drifting inchoate in other people's minds" (The Times-London), "Samuel Huntington is a professor of Harvard University, a noted scholar and the author of the global bestseller, *The Clash of Civilizations and the Remaking of World Order*" (The Economist), "Samuel Huntington is the author of the most important works of political science of this generation" (The Weekly Standard). What is more is that our current realities seem to fit Huntington's dire warnings. We do seem, after September 11, to be in a clash of civilizations against peoples of morally inferior gods, religions, and societies. In this way, Huntington reinforces a simplistic and dualistic worldview—one where something is either black or white, sacred or profane. Thus in a world already laden with horrendous cultural, racial, and religious conflicts, Huntington only puts us more at each other's throats.

On The Origins Of Being Other

But what about people like me that pose such a threat to the world? What about us that is so terrifying? Why is Huntington blaming us for all that is wrong with the world? The answer, of course, is that we are supposedly morally inferior. This is why we supposedly have morally inferior gods, religions, cultures, and societies. This is also why we supposedly procreate without any regard to what we or the world can afford. Apparently, our moral inferiority resides at the core of our being. We therefore cannot be engaged as civilized human beings who respond to reason. We must be coerced, threatened, harassed, intimidated, and legislated against. We must, in other worlds, be dealt with like savages and barbarians.

But how did we become deserving of this characterization? For instance, I oppose any manner of violence and prejudice. I believe all communities and societies are morally obligated to care for those among them who are weak and vulnerable. I also believe in a god of infinite love and mercy and in a world where vengeance has no place. Yet Huntington still insists on portraying me as a threat to all that is good and just. He insists that I bear the burden of being morally inferior. He even has no qualms of acknowledging that he has no friends, neighbors, and colleagues who are Latinos. But in reality, I am merely an artifact of Huntington's deepest anxieties and insecurities. I am born out of his inability to embrace the world's ambiguity, complexity, and mystery. He is therefore afraid of me. I terrify him. He therefore aspires to destroy my own ambiguity, complexity, and mystery by demanding that I fit into his simplistic and dualistic worldview. That is, that I stop being Brown—the color of creation.

The paranoia found in *Who We Are* suggests that Huntington is becoming increasingly desperate. He no doubt believes that my victory is near. His worse fears are on the brink of coming through. The barbarians and savages are threatening to rule the world. The reign of anarchy and chaos is about to begin. Thus whereas *Clash of Civilizations* was about protecting the West from the barbarians and savages, *Who We Are* shows a fallback to now just protecting the US. Apparently, the rest of the West has been lost to the forces of postcolonialism and cosmopolitanism as a result of the "flood" of immigrants from Africa and the Middle East. For Huntington, we are now on the verge of the final great battle. He must therefore now write—in *Who We Are*—as a "scholar and patriot," "deeply concerned about the unity and strength of my country based on liberty, equality, law, and individual rights." We are to believe that the US, with its Protestant values and beliefs, is now all that stands between the rule of reason, civility, and decency, and that of ignorance, chaos, and anarchy.

It is unfortunate that Huntington understands the world in this dire way. It is even much more unfortunate that he has the means and access to impose this understanding on so much of the world, especially in the face of September 11. It constitutes such a tragic view of the world. Fortunately, however, more and more of us are refusing to bear the burden that Huntington wishes to impose on us. We actually believe in the possibility of new and different worlds. We are, as Gloria Anzaldúa beautifully describes us, the *new mestizas*. Indeed, what distinguishes us from Huntington is our belief that the world is laden with much potentiality, fecundity, and beauty. We embrace the world's ambiguity, complexity, and mystery, which is also to say that we believe the world lends for infinite possibilities. We therefore believe in a storied world—one where we are inherently story creating and story consuming beings. Through stories we frame, organize, and make sense of our worlds. We believe that we are shot through with stories and that stories precede and exceed us. Yet for us it is our storied nature that makes the world so compelling and fascinating. For no story is inherently complete. That is, no story lends for one meaning, one interpretation, one truth, even one experience. Stories are inherently unstable and incomplete. They change and evolve. They even devolve and die. Stories are therefore inherently elastic. Yet because they are inherently elastic they are inherently democratic, in the sense of promoting diverse understandings, meanings, and experiences.

Religions, sciences, cultures, and paradigms are all stories. Each represents a set of various stories of how the world is and how the world should be. What Huntington is giving us is a story of the world. He is no doubt entitled to this story. But in the end, this is merely one story among many. However, what should really concern us most are the implications and consequences that come with different stories, as well as the origins of different stories. For instance, Does this story expand our understanding and experiencing of the world? Where is this story coming from? Why are we creating this story now? What is this story's appeal? Why is this story appealing to us now? To whom is this story appealing to and why? But again, we are to believe that Huntington is supposedly giving us the Truth, the harsh reality. His description—really interpretation—of the world is beyond and outside of history, culture, and ideology. That is, unbound from all that is flesh and human. We even read in reviews of *Who We Are* that Huntington offers "clear thinking" and "a tough-minded evaluation." "Huntington also convincingly demonstrates." "Glib, politically correct talk finds no place in Huntington's analysis, and for that readers should be grateful." "Huntington marshals a body of evidence to support his claims."

Huntington believes in a finite world, where only one set of realities is ultimately permissible. This is why, for instance, Huntington champions assimilation and adherence to a fixed set of cultural and political precepts. For Huntington, culture is a premodern and primitive notion. It is what you have before you have science and the various institutions that promote science and are based on science. It is presumably the embrace of science—which supposedly makes for the elevation of reason over passion—that distinguishes the US and the West from the rest of the world. Thus Huntington wants to hear nothing about meanings and interpretations. He wants to hear of only truths and facts. He believes that it is the intrusion of culture—thanks to those he contemptuously refers to as postcolonialists and postmodernists—upon the hegemony of science that most threatens the integrity of the US by undermining our pursuit and belief in *Truth*. He is appalled that such intrusions and incursions are actually coming from within the walls of the most elite academic institutions. Then again, such is the pending fall that the US apparently faces if it is unable to halt the march of multiculturalism, cosmopolitanism, and postcolonialism.

So once again Huntington continues to insist that we look

at the world in a dualistic and simplistic way. In this case, between those who believe in science and reason and those who believe in culture and passion. We must take sides and swear allegiances. But more and more of us refuse to do either, for, again, we look at the world differently to Huntington. Our view of the world is much more layered, much more textured, much more nuanced. In fact, Huntington gives us a false and dangerous schism, and thereby pushes us to take sides in ways that only further alienate and distance us from each other.

The Power of Illusions

Huntington would like us to believe that the US is an Anglo-Protestant nation. It is one story. We supposedly reject this story at our own peril. But the US has never been linguistically, culturally, ethnically, ideologically, culturally, religiously, or racially stable. It has always been richly diverse, that is, richly storied. Moreover, this diversity permeates all communities, ethnicities, nationalities, societies, races, cultures, and religions in the US.

Yet Huntington insists on making us believe that all of this diversity is absent. He no doubt believes that diversity and complexity undermine the stability and homogeneity that are supposedly vital for progress and social evolution. But diversity, rather than homogeneity, is the order of all naturally occurring ecologies. In fact, all naturally occurring ecologies evolve towards diversity and complexity. This is how such ecologies survive and prosper. Diversity and complexity make ecologies resilient and creative. Still, Huntington, in the face of this harsh reality, continues to believe otherwise. He therefore continues to see homogeneity where there is diversity, stability where there is instability, and simplicity where there is complexity. "The American people who achieved independence in the late eighteenth century were few and homogenous: overwhelmingly white thanks [!] to the exclusion of blacks and Indians from citizenship" (emphasis mine). Moreover, Huntington continues to believe that diversity poses a threat to the US. "The extent and nature of [Latino] immigration differ fundamentally from those of previous immigration, and the assimilation successes of the past are unlikely to be duplicated with the contemporary flood of immigrants from Latin America. This reality poses a fundamental question: Will the United States remain a country with a single national language and a core Anglo-Protestant culture? By ignoring this question, Americans acquiesce to their eventual transformation into two peoples with two cultures (Anglo and Hispanic) and two languages (English and Spanish)."

But there is no Anglo-Protestant culture, just as much as there is no Latino culture. There are Anglo-Protestant cultures and Latino cultures. But Huntington sees none of the beauty and hope that comes with our different cultures mingling and converging. He is unable to even once escape his anxieties and insecurities. He demands, even in the face of slavery, Jim Crow, the near extinction of Native Americans, and other such evils that remarkably find no mention in *Who We Are*, that "Americans . . . recommit themselves to the Anglo-Protestant culture, traditions, and values that for three and half centuries have been embraced by Americans of all races, ethnicities, and religions and that have been the source of their liberty, unity, power, prosperity, and moral leadership as a force for good in the world." We must, in other words, remain beholden to the past. We too must be afraid of the world's ambiguity, complexity, and mystery. We too must believe, even in the face of our own historical misery, that without an Anglo-Protestant culture the US will descend into chaos and anarchy. We too must therefore concur that "There is much that is valuable in Mr. Huntington's work, which represents a real effort to address threats to social cohesion and to recover useful knowledge about a culture all but eclipsed in our time" (Washington Times). We must also be "glad that a scholar like Huntington has raised these issues, since they deserve serious consideration" (Slate). For "Once again, Huntington is arrestingly right about the challenges facing liberal democracy that many liberals have been loath to acknowledge" (Los Angeles Times)

But evolution unfolds towards the future, towards the unknown, towards the edge of chaos. This is why evolution requires courage—the willingness to risk life. Yet without evolution, life perishes. For what evolution constitutes is possibility—the possibility of something new and better emerging from within the world's ambiguity. Huntington makes believe that the US is up against various forces that threaten its ideological and cultural integrity. But the US is really up against the forces of evolution—forces that are ultimately pushing the US to become more expansive and inclusive. We can no doubt interrupt and harass these forces. But such a project does nothing good for us. For evolution is beyond us. Its impulse belongs to life itself.

The world is doubt on a march towards more and more diversity and complexity. Our commonly held notions of race, ethnicity, sexuality, gender, spirituality, and geography are all collapsing and imploding, and as a result, making our world increasingly diverse, complex, and ambiguous. Indeed, the world has never before seen so much diversity and complexity. We have always been able to fit each other into various boxes and categories. But now the world, in every which way, is becoming more and more Brown.

Moreover, more and more of us are determined to defy boxes and categories, a practice, of course, that Huntington finds most vexing. We insist on moving between worlds. However, for us, moving between worlds is much more than simply physically moving between worlds, or even embracing the different worlds from which we originally came. To move between worlds is to move beyond the worlds that are behind us as well as those that are before us. In other words, to move between worlds is to move towards new conceptual, epistemological, and theoretical worlds—those which we have only begun to imagine.

There is no doubt a primal side to be human. This is the side that is afraid of the world's ambiguity, complexity, and mystery. The side that is seduced by homogeneity, stability, and simplicity. The side that believes in competition and aggression. The side that focuses on self-preservation. But this primal side merely constitutes one side of what it means to be human. We possess other sides—sides that are moral, cultural, existential, emotional, historical, relational, social, sensual, and, yes, even spiritual. Huntington, of course, never speaks to these other sides. He insists on portraying us as being no better than animals—driven by purely primal instincts and impulses. He has no faith in our capacity to act decently without elaborate structures of order, control, and coercion. He believes hierarchy is inevitable because we lack any capacity for moral development. He therefore expects and sees only the worse in us.

But we can control our primal instincts and impulses. Hierarchy is no way inevitable. We can be more merciful, more compassionate, more selfless, more tolerant. We can create communities and societies that distribute resources more evenly and generously. We can also create communities and societies that are much more diverse and democratic. But Huntington says nothing about our better experiences in being human. He continues to see in us only that which is ugly. Indeed, there is much within us that is ugly, and much of history seems to make a compelling case about us being devoid of any moral capacity. But just as well, history also shows that there is much potential for beauty in us.

So whereas Huntington would like us to believe that we are in a death struggle with other peoples, other cultures, other religions, and ultimately other civilizations, we need to keep in mind that this framing only serves to deny the real struggle that is before us and has always been before us. What is more is that this diversion encourages us to deal with the struggle in ways that are ultimately catastrophic. For if the struggle we face is within us, and against an opponent that we can never really destroy, then aggression can never be seen as a viable option. We must do something else, and something else quickly.

Our Storied Worlds

The notion of us being storied beings in a storied world is quite heuristic. It allows for a highly expansive description of the human condition and all of the complexity, diversity, and mystery that comes with being human. Yet this notion does more than describes. It allows us to reframe and revision what it means to be human in a world that will always be larger than us. It is also a deeply organic notion. Through stories we make sense of the world and order our lives. It is also through stories we trade our experiences and organize that which seems unorganizable. In fact, our story-creating, story-consuming, story-trading proclivity reveals a lot of what it means to be human. No other species possess the capacity to construct the complex kinds of stories we are capable of constructing, and regardless of how sophisticated technology ever becomes, no machine will ever—ever—be able to produce stories that are remotely textured, nuanced, and layered as ours. Our redemption therefore resides in our stories, as only through stories and our ability to create stories we realize our ability to help complete the world.

We can impose any story on the world. Yet the fact that we can do so in no way means that all stories are morally equal. Indeed, what is probably most appealing about a narrative stance is the recognition that the world does possess a moral capacity. Stories that promote life lend for elaborate interpretations—interpretations that expand our understanding and experiencing of the world. This, in fact, is where Huntington's story collapses. It makes no demands on us. Also, stories that lack the ability to change and evolve puts us at odds with the world by blocking us from appreciating how our fates are intertwined as a result of us being of an interconnected and interdependent world. In this way, morally superior narratives always push us to engage the world in much more expansive and inclusive ways as our well-being is inseparable from everything that is of this world.

Final Thoughts

We should always be suspicious of any attempt to impose one story on the world. On the other hand, the evolving and changing nature of the world will never allow any story to achieve this goal. There will always be emerging stories, converging stories, and disappearing stories. Our redemption resides in communities and societies that forever promote the evolution of new stories. We should therefore be committed to the celebration of stories and the conditions and practices that promote new and different stories.

But we are all stories. We all articulate a story of how the world is and how it should be. In every moment of being we forge and articulate our stories. However, the world, as a result of our spaces and distances increasingly collapsing and imploding, seems to be upon the dawn of a new genre of stories. I am referring to the complexity, universality, and hope found in these emergent stories—the ones that are increasingly being generated by those of us who move between worlds. Still, those who insist on imposing one story on the world remain at our throats. Thus our struggle is really a struggle for stories. For as stories we all carry within ourselves all that is potentially good and beautiful in the world. Let us therefore be stories that tell of the coming of new and better worlds.

IV
Our Deep Prejudices

Everyday many human beings are savagely beaten, mutilated, and killed for simply being of a different race, ethnicity, sexual orientation, religion, and nationality. In response to the usual outrage over reports of such heinous crimes, many states in the U.S. and the federal government now have hate crime laws. Such laws allow for harsher punishments for crimes that are directly related to a person's race, nationality, sexual orientation, ethnicity, gender, and religion. Supposedly, the fact that the origin of the killing or beating is related to a person's difference makes for a distinction in the savagery. The general sentiment among proponents of hate crime legislation is that the harsher provisions will act as a deterrent.

Hate crimes, whether directed against one individual, many people or the property of a particular group, should be anathema to a free and open society that values and cherishes individual rights and freedom. Perpetrators of hate crimes are determined to send a message that the victims are fair targets because of who they are. . . Critics of hate crimes legislation, many of whom write disparagingly from ivory towers far removed from the real life experience of helping the victims of these crimes, use creative prose to dismiss these laws. . . .

When law enforcement lacks guidelines and laws designed to address these types of crime, enforcement becomes inconsistent. . . .

One result is that the victim and his or her community becomes distrustful of and alienated from law enforcement, sometimes resorting to vigilantism or retaliatory acts to avenge the indignities suffered. Instead of cooperative efforts between disenfranchised people and the legal system, mistrust is fostered and tensions can be exacerbated. Hate crime statutes, contrary to critics, do not increase conflict between races, genders and nationality groups but rather have led to extraordinary partnerships among civil rights groups, law enforcement agencies and state and local governments. Police-community relations have improved in many localities where law enforcement officials have shown a commitment to being tough on hate criminals and sensitive to their victims. At this point in history, New York could surely benefit from such a partnership.

Howie Katz, Director of the New York Regional Office of the Anti-Defamation League and Chairman of the New York State Hate Crimes Bill Coalition

Prominent proponents of hate crime legislation contend that a civilized society has a moral, political, legal, and social responsibility to do whatever is necessary to stop such heinous crimes. Legislatures are particularly anxious to pass harsh hate crime laws, especially after prominent reports of a person being savagely beaten to death because (supposedly) of that person's differences. Persons of all political and social stripes tend to adamantly support such legislation.

For all our documentation of these crimes and others, our political and moral disgust at them, our morbid fascination with them, our sensitivity to their social meaning, we seem at times to have no better idea now than we ever

had of what exactly they were about. About what that moment means when, for some reason or other, one human being asserts absolute, immutable superiority over another. About not the violence, but what the violence expresses. About what exactly hate is. And what our own part in it may be.

Andrew Sullivan
The New York Times Magazine
September 26, 1999

Reasonable minds cannot dispute that something needs to be done to cure the social ill of hate crime. A person who commits a crime against another person solely because of the victim's race, religion or some other characteristic must be punished with the same vehemence with which the offender pursued the victim. However, hate crime legislation is not the proper means to achieve this goal. Our Bill of Rights forms the cornerstone of our democracy. If democracy is left to work as it was originally intended, hate crime will arouse the good majority to reject those wrongdoers and grow stronger in the ever-present struggle between good and evil. The integrity of our Constitution must be considered first and foremost in drafting legislation and there currently does not exist hate crime legislation that does not compromise the integrity of the First Amendment.

John Morgenstern, Esq.

Hate crime legislation makes for interesting bedfellows. Members of disenfranchised and marginalized groups demand that hate crimes legislation be passed so as to put a halt to such crimes. Hate crimes legislation is seen as progress. Such groups use such legislation as a kind of big stick on a society that is stubbornly resisting the notion of full equality for all human beings. On the other hand, persons of the dominant groups are also anxious to support such legislation so as to show the status quo's disgust with such crimes. Such groups use hate crime legislation as a way of showing that bigotry is a phenomenon of the past. Support for hate crime legislation is a new litmus test for good politics.

It has been a source of shame that year after year New York State has failed to enact a meaningful hate-crime law even as violence against gays and ministry groups has become more common. . . .

This week the State Senate finally approved a bill that will increase punishments for those convicted of crimes motivated by hatred. These lawmakers are sending an important message that such crimes harm entire communicates as well as individual victims, and therefore deserve greater punishment. The Senate bill would increase sentences significantly for crimes in which the victims are singled out because of their race, gender, religion, age, disability or sexual orientation. . . .

It is time New York took a strong step against violence directed toward specific groups.
Editorial, The New York Times
June 9, 2000

The reality is that hate crime legislation makes for cheap moral currency. Compared to the gains that the status quo acquires from supporting such legislation, such legislation asks nothing much—really nothing at all—from us. The reason being that such legislation never calls us to interrogate our own biases against persons who are of a different race, ethnicity, gender, sexual orientation, nationality, and so forth. Fervent support of such legislation can even make for the illusion that such biases and prejudices no longer exist. Such legislation therefore calls us to risk no life. We are never challenged to look at our own complicity in creating a context that promotes these crimes.

The truth is, the distinction between a crime filled with personal hate and a crime filled with group hate is an essentially arbitrary one. It tells us nothing interesting about the psychological contours of the specific actor or his specific victim. It is a function primarily of politics, of special interest groups carving out particular protections for themselves, rather than a serious response to a serious criminal concern. In such an endeavor, hate-crime-law advocates cram an entire world of human motivations into an immutable, tiny box called hate, and hope to have solved a problem. But nothing has been solved; and some harm may even have been done.

In an attempt to repudiate a past that treated people differently because of the color of their skin, or their sex, or religion or sexual orientation, we may merely create a future that permanently treats people differently because of the color of their skin, or their sex, religion or sexual orientation. This notion of a hate crime, and the concept of hate that lies behind it, takes a psychological mystery and turns it into a facile political artifact. Rather than compounding this error and extending it even further, we should seriously consider repealing the concept altogether.

Andrew Sullivan
The New York Times Magazine
September 26, 1999

The basic problem with which all proposed hate-crime laws must contend is that they create a legal distinction between someone who kills a gay man because he hates gays and someone who kills a gas-station attendant in order to steal from his cash register. To create such a distinction in effect penalizes some criminals more harshly, not because of their deeds, but because of their beliefs. This clashes with constitutional principles protecting free thought and equality under the law. . . .

> *When hate crimes occur, they should be identified and reported, as legislation already on the books requires. The criminals should be dealt with just as harshly as every other kind of criminal. What's needed now is not a knee-jerk reaction by Congress and the states. Fundamentally, bigotry against gays is a cultural issue, to be tackled through the determined pursuit of attitudinal change. What's needed now, then, is loud and principled condemnation of the malicious murder of Matthew Shepard and of the festering bigotry that motivated it.*
> Editorial, The New Republic
> November 22, 1998

The hate crime legislation project is morally, theoretically, and politically bankrupt. It is particularly unfortunate that members of marginalized and disenfranchised groups enthusiastically support such legislation and use such legislation as a measure of progress. I am by no means downplaying the reality that each day many human beings are savagely beaten and often killed for simply being a different race, sexually orientation, and so forth. Neither do I deny the possibility that such legislation does deter a certain amount of bestiality. Even one beating is one too many. Understandably, persons of disenfranchised and marginalized groups are afraid of being savagely beaten to death. I understand this fear only too well. However, the point that I am trying to make is that the focus on passing and enforcing such legislation so as to promote the good society is misplaced. We are again fighting with shadows.

Crime & Punishment

The bedrock assumption in hate crime legislation is that

Diversity

punishment and coercion can fashion moral behavior. We presumably can be deterred from certain behaviors with enough coercion and punishment. Consequently, after prominent reports of savagery, all groups call for even harsher punitive provisions. We look at the problem in terms of punishment or the lack thereof. This approach to human behavior assumes that human beings have to be equipped with morality. We are supposedly without any. It is supposedly the responsibility of society—by whatever means necessary—to equip us with moral codes. We supposedly have a proclivity for chaos and destruction. Consequently, a civilized society is supposedly characterized by the development of complex institutions and mechanisms to control and suppress this proclivity. We focus on which institutions equip us best with moral codes. We ultimately have to be coerced, controlled, equipped, deterred, stopped, and often punished so as to act decently. Presumably, by exercising the necessary order and control, passing the proper legislation, hates crimes will be deterred. Hate crimes supposedly result from the lack of institutional control, the kind of control that is necessary to control our supposed proclivity for animality. We cast hate crimes as institutional problems demanding institutional solutions. Consequently, our focus is always on fixing the legislation, tightening legal loopholes, adding new punishment provisions, or simply extending legislation to give other marginalized groups legal protection. In the end, both elites of wealth and power and members of historically marginalized groups are relying on institutions to make for a good society.

But our faith in the potentiality of institutions to bring forth the good society is misplaced. Punishment legitimizes the status quo. It legitimizes hierarchy by reinforcing the view that we supposedly have a proclivity for chaos and devolution that needs to be inorganically (institutionally) controlled. In other words, punishment reinforces our deep distrust and suspicion of our humanity. It maintains a necessary fear that sustains our subordination to the forces of domination and exploitation. Punishment also sustains the status quo by limiting our humanity. Punishment demands nothing much from us. It demands no risking of life. It also requires no deepening of our capacity to love, trust, or to exercise deep levels of compassion and understanding. It never challenges us to deepen our humanity and thereby end the bestiality that is often related to the expression of our differences. Persons who are generally committed to ending the many violent crimes against persons of different races and so forth must also be committed to ending all forms of punishment and coercion. But only a few persons are actually willing to do so. So hate crime legislation gives most of us cheap moral currency. Such legislation poses no threat to the status quo.

Crimes of Hate

It is commonly assumed that hate crimes are about race, gender, sexual orientation, and so forth. Such crimes are supposedly about a lack of toleration of the differences of others. We appear determined to want the matter to be seen this way. No doubt, this narrow focus works well for most of us. This kind of focus poses no threat to the status quo. But hate crimes have nothing to do with race, ethnicity, and so forth. Such crimes even have nothing to do with toleration, or even hate. Hate is a natural human emotion. We all hate. Yet, on the other hand, most of us will never violently harm others for simply being different. Hate crimes are fundamentally about violence. Such crimes are born of a social system that fosters violence. To look at hate crimes in terms of race, toleration, and hate, is to miss the context to which such crimes belong. Again, although all of us hate, most of us will never act on such hate to the extent of physically harming a next person. It takes a certain context to legitimize such hate. That context is obviously one that fosters violence. In other words, looking at hate crimes in relation to race, toleration, and so forth deflects scrutiny of how violent is our society. Indeed, a society that fosters competition rather than cooperation is a violent society. A society that fosters deception, distrust, suspicion, and apathy rather than transparency, hope, understanding, and compassion is equally violent. I also understand that most persons of a hierarchical society would never commit hate crimes. I am in no way trying to shift responsibility away from human beings. We have volition, and this capacity comes with responsibility. Ultimately, all of us have to be held accountable for our actions or lack thereof. I would never want it any other way. The point that I am trying to make here is that hate crimes mask the deep levels of violence that our society generates.

We now have a high threshold for violence. We are increasingly devoid of any deep sensitivity to our fragility. This lack of sensitivity is seen in the increasing transfer of wealth from the many to the few at the top, making for an ever-widening gap between rich and poor. It is also seen in our indifference to the poor and downtrodden, the marginalized and disenfranchised, the homeless, the delinquent, and the weak. On the other hand, our increasing insensitivity is probably most evident in our determination to legally punish children as adults.

The hate crimes that make the evening news scare us. Most often, the cruelty and savagery that characterize such crimes is difficult to bear. We are anxious to disconnect ourselves from such cruelty and savagery. The common belief is that only animals could commit such heinous crimes. The passing of hate crime legislation shows a kind of cleansing of self. Such legislation shows us attempting to quiet our own biases and prejudices.

Hate crimes reflect the actions of human beings who have lost any kind of sensitivity to the humanity of others. Such persons are by no means the exception. Any society that engenders the level of violence that our society fosters will consistently make for such persons. Many persons will go from low levels of sensitivity to no kind of sensitivity. Race, gender, and other differences will naturally appear as a pretext as our society already fosters deep biases and prejudices about those differences. We deflect attention of the origin of the cruelty so as to deflect our own responsibility. We want the attention to be confined to a select group of persons—the supposed deviants and delinquents. We want a group that to focus our anger and disgust on. We want the matter to be seen in terms of race, ethnicity, and so forth. We want any serious scrutiny to escape us. We want no interrogation of our ways of being.

Legitimizing The Status Quo

The status quo needs hate crime laws for a variety of reasons. Proponents insist that hate crimes warrant a different set of laws. Such laws supposedly act as a symbol of negation against such crimes, though many scholars and legal theorists quarrel with both the constitutionality and usefulness of hate crime legislation. The fact of the matter is that the status quo needs hate crimes. It needs any commotion that will deflect attention away from the forces of exploitation and domination. It needs to busy us, to undercut moments and occasions for reflection and contemplation. Hate crimes legislation also legitimizes the status quo by showing its rejection of what is commonly seen as evil and heinous acts. Moreover, hate crimes resolidify the bedrock belief that human beings have a proclivity for chaos and destruction. The status quo is seen as combating this proclivity through harsh legislation.

Hate crimes foster our dependency on the status quo. That is, hate crimes legislation relegitimizes the notion that institutions make for the good society. Even scholars and legal theorists who are against hate crimes legislation insist that only harsh laws can remedy the problem. Obviously, both opponents and proponents of such legislation are working with a common set of assumptions. Both look at hate crimes as about hate. Both also believe that legislation can remedy the problem. We exploit the anxiety that comes with hate crimes. Hate crimes make for rallying occasions. We rally around the status quo. We call loudly for new legislation, new amendments, and new protections. We look to our institutions to end the problem. We demand swift action. In rallying around the status quo, our dependency on institutions increases. We are less willing to consider our own ways of being and experiencing the world. Our fears of the world heighten. It becomes increasingly difficult for us to consider the possibility of noninstitutional solutions to our problems. In other words, in becoming increasingly dependent on institutions, we become increasingly dependent on hierarchy. The result is only the worsening of the problem as hierarchy only fosters dysfunctionality; in turn, this worsening situation only further increases our dependency on institutions and hierarchy. This spiral phenomenon is aptly seen in the evolution of hate crimes.

Hate crimes are by no means a new human phenomenon.

Race, gender, ethnicity, and so forth have always been related to murder and mutilation. The history of the world is largely a history of hate crimes. Only the concept of hate crimes is relatively new. The evolution of the concept reflects the reality that many persons are using race, gender, and sexual orientation, and so forth to justify the murder and mutilation of other human beings. The figures show that such crimes are increasing. Many contend that this reality is merely a fallout from a world that is increasingly laden with all kinds of differences. That is, different peoples are now forced to deal with each other. Hate crimes supposedly reflect the actions of persons who lack the sophistication to deal with this new world. Others contend that hate crimes reflect the changing power relations in the world. Members of historically dominant groups are contesting the newfound power and rise of historically marginalized and disenfranchised groups. Hate crimes are supposedly acts of intimidation and subjugation.

But neither explanation gives us a compelling account of what is commonly referred to as hate crimes. The rise of hate crimes is entwined with the rise of other kinds of violent crimes. We are witnessing an increasing rise in violent behavior across the board. As such, any solid explanation of the origin of hate crimes must also account for the rise of other markings of dysfunctionality. In short, any explanation that only focuses on hate crimes is shallow. Indeed, no one disputes the notion that hate crimes reflect dysfunctionality, regardless of how broad dysfunctionality is defined. But shallow explanations are what the status quo gives us. The rise of criminality and mental disease is left out of the equation. Hate crimes are reduced to problems of diversity rather than problems of dysfunctionality. In sum, by controlling how the problem is defined and understood, the status quo controls how the problem is managed and resolved. However, by controlling the problem this way, the status quo ultimately controls us.

Arguably, a better explanation of this steady rise of dysfunctionality can be found in the spiral relation between our dependency on institutions and hierarchy. We have already seen that hierarchy fosters dysfunctionality. Consequently, any society that is increasingly dependent on hierarchy will reflect increasing levels of dysfunctionality. We will find a society that is increasingly homicidal and suicidal. We will find newfound expressions of savagery and cruelty. We will also find a widening gap between rich and poor, high levels of distrust, suspicion, apathy, and fear, and a society that desires information rather than communication, networks rather than friendships, and suburbs rather than neighborhoods. Further, we will find a privileging of private over public spaces. We will also find a society that is materially rather than spiritually driven, and increasing levels of fragmentation, separation, and division. We will find, in sum, a society that is increasingly less human.

Love & Hate

We never consider seriously the option of love to deal with the increasing levels of hate that permeates our society. Then again, love assumes human beings have a potentiality for goodness. It assumes that most of our problems result from ways of being that obstruct the evolution of our moral, existential, and spiritual strives. Of course, love promotes relations that foster empathy rather than apathy, trust rather than distrust, transparency rather than deception, courage rather than fear, equality rather than inequality, and selflessness rather than selfishness. In sum, love undermines hierarchy. In so doing, love poses a direct threat to the status quo by delegitimizing all the beliefs, values, assumptions, and practices that the status quo thrives on.

We remain of the belief that hate crimes can be stopped with enough coercion and punishment. The solution to hate crimes is assumed to be institutional, meaning that the solution resides in our institutions rather than with us. Lost within this kind of reasoning is the fact that hate crimes merely manifest a much deeper problem. Any society that undercuts love fosters animality and bestiality. Hate crimes reflect this move towards animality. Hate crimes show us being less human. Such crimes reflect relations that obstruct our moral, existential, and spiritual strives. Hate crimes are symptoms of human dysfunctionality. The fact that such crimes are increasing only means that many of us are becoming less and less human. Yet, on the other hand, what emerges from this lessening of our humanity only reinforces the status-quo's great claim that human beings have a proclivity for chaos and social devolution and, as a result, need rigid and complex institutions.

To view hate crimes as symptoms of human dysfunctionality by no means represents an attempt to downplay the barbarism and cruelty that characterize such crimes. Instead, the aim is to better understand the origins of the forces that make for a society that increasingly fosters hate crimes. In my opinion, to look at hate crimes as fundamentally about a society that undercuts the expansion of our humanity helps us to better understand the gravity and urgency of this evil that bedevils us.

Love as a remedy to human dysfunctionality is probably the oldest of teachings. All prophets relate love to redemption and salvation. Our own salvation and redemption is dependent upon us expanding our capacity to love. This expansion reflects our becoming fully human. It manifests the evolution of human relations that are laden with trust, transparency, and compassion. Hate undercuts our redemption and salvation. It destroys life and thereby limits our humanity. Suffice to say, hate demands no deep exercising of our humanity. It calls us to risk no life. It is, again, no doubt a natural emotion. It gives definition to the other forces that are of the world. Hate defines love, just as much as apathy defines empathy, and fear defines courage. Hate is of the world. It gives our humanity depth and complexity. We can never end hate. Hate is always of us. It will always dwell within us. Our goal must be to move beyond hate, to limit hate.

Love heals us by promoting union and communion rather than separation and fragmentation. It exercises all of our humanity. It always calls us to risk life. As such, to love is difficult. Tribulations are always at hand. The prophets tell us this again and again. Yet we all obligated to expand our humanity by loving deeper and better. It is only through the expansion of our humanity that the goodness of our potentiality is realized. In other words, only through the expansion of our humanity we realize the love that is necessary to bring completion to the world. The fact that hate increasingly pervades our ways of being should deeply concern us. We are losing our humanity. But hate crimes are merely symptoms of this reality. Other symptoms abound, such as the increasing inequality that pervades our society, the rise of materialism and consumerism, the rise of global capitalism, the deification of a hierarchical ethos, the deification of competition, the increasing reliance on vengeance for justice, and our increasing indifference to the world's marginalized and disenfranchised peoples.

The status quo thrives on fostering practices that make the evolution of love difficult. We are beholden to a status quo that perilously threatens our humanity, our redemption and salvation. The status quo needs us to be indifferent to the marginalized and disenfranchised. This system only rewards the selfish. The status quo also needs us to accept inequality as simply the way of the world. In doing so, most of us come to have no problem with the increasing inequality that pervades the world. Supposedly, this inequality reflects the best and brightness rising *naturally* to the top and claiming most of the wealth and power.

The status quo has also managed to get us to accept competition as the order of the world. It is supposedly a world of zero/sum games. It is a world of distrust and suspicion. Survival is dependent upon besting, even destroying, opponents. Supposedly, attending to the poor and the meek weakens the survival of the rich and the strong, a practice that ultimately threatens to bring about the downfall of all humanity. Supposedly, a natural culling of the meek is vital for the evolution of humanity. This is what many now view as compassion. We now accept all of these positions as given, as truths given to us by the gods themselves. Such is our faith, our conviction. Such is also our estrangement from our humanity. We are convinced that human beings have a proclivity for chaos and devolution and view hierarchy as vital to the evolution of the good society. Indeed, our history is violent and bloody. We are, most of all, losing nearly all of our faith in our humanity. Increasingly, nihilism and fatalism grip our consciousness of the world. Hope eludes us. Our ways of being are increasingly laden with despair, distrust, apathy, and suspicion. Our children are increasingly massacring other children. Evidently, our humanity is beginning to bottom out.

Hate crimes make for a good diversion. We rally around the status quo with gusto. But what is the cost of this diversion? To begin with, our diagnosis is wrong, making for wrong solutions to the problem. Again, hate crimes have nothing to do with our differences, and legislation offers no end to such behaviors. Further, this wrong diagnosis only legitimizes the status quo that makes for hate crimes. In addition, this diagnosis masks the deep and perilous levels of dysfunctionality that the status quo creates. In doing so, this diagnosis delimits the extent of our culpability and responsibility for remedying the solution. By making no demands of us, that is, demanding no risking of life, this diagnosis legitimizes the status quo by explicitly limiting human action and responsibility. But the matter that must concern us the most is the hopelessness that this diagnosis perpetuates. Hopeless human beings pose no threat to the status quo. Hopelessness only fuels despair and misery. It makes us indifferent to those who are marginalized and disenfranchised, indifferent to peoples who are different and who often reflect different ways of being and experiencing the world, indifferent to the condition of the planet and the condition of the world, and, worse of all, indifferent to the condition of our own humanity. Indifference makes us less human. It makes us subservient to the forces of domination and exploitation. In making us less human, however, the status quo perilously threatens the well being of the world. This is the real cost of pursuing a diversion. Hate crimes are shadows. It is our being less human that cast such hideous shadows.

Final Thoughts

Leaving uninterrogated the assumption that human beings possess a proclivity for chaos and devolution blocks any possibility of a genuinely new and different discussion of human potentiality. That is, this assumption subtly limits our understanding of what being human being means. The result being that this assumption limits human action and responsibility. It retards our exploration of new and different ways of experiencing the world by promoting fear rather than hope. Moreover, this assumption fosters fear, despair, and apathy. It makes us afraid of each other and of our own humanity. The result being the evolution of human relations laden with distrust, deception, and fear. The result is also dependency, that is, our dependency on institutions, structures, and laws to fix our many problems. We make no connection between the evolution of such problems and the relations that bound such problems. Instead, such problems are seen as rising from our defects, our supposed lack of perfection and goodness. To view hate crimes as deviancy also misses the sacred relation between our actions—and lack thereof—and the condition of the world. In my view, this is arguably the most significant omission. This omission limits our understanding of ethics and morality by ultimately limiting our understanding of the world.

Love tells us much about the potential of our humanity as about the potentiality of the world. Love also tells us a lot about our obligation to others as well as the world. In expanding human action, and by that expanding our experiencing of the world, love reveals and deepens our obligation to the world, each other, and our humanity. Love nourishes the world. It brings completion to the world and to our humanity. In short, love heals us. It makes us whole.

It is out lack of understanding of our connection to the world that is what perilously threatens our humanity the most. It is also what most exposes the weakness of the morality and ethics that are set by the status quo. Our actions do affect the condition of the world. This much is undisputed. Consequently, our ethics must commit us to practices that at least bring no harm upon the world. In my view, this benchmark offers a solid beginning to build a new ethics. We only have to acknowledge that the world and us are of one consciousness, one potentiality.

Love is about revolution. To love is to transgress—to transgress the status quo, to transgress the stability of our own being, our own humanity. Love makes for new ways of being in the world. This is what makes love a threat to the status quo. Love expands human action. It undercuts the fear and suspicion that the status quo thrives on. Love enlightens and deepens our humanity. It lessens the threats of our differences. It also undermines our separation from the marginalized and disenfranchised, the poor and downtrodden, and others who reflect different ways of being and experiencing the world. In sum, love fosters union rather than separation. It undermines hierarchy and our dependency on institutions, structures, and laws.

Love turns us towards each other. Yet, to love is difficult. Love stretches our humanity. It comes with all kinds of tribulations. It is never any easy. On the other hand, however, love is the only path to redemption and salvation. It is the only path to ending the barbarism that comes with being less human. It is also the only path to ending a status quo that blocks our becoming fully human.

V

On Differences & Diversity

We all hold to systems of beliefs and values that view certain practices as good and others as wrong. Such systems give definitions to our humanity. To accept and respect certain practices simply shatters the integrity of our beliefs and value systems. Understanding this predicament, proponents of identity politics tell us that toleration stretches our humanity. It supposedly makes us better human beings. Also, toleration supposedly makes for a better society, especially one that is increasingly diverse and multicultural. Proponents of identity politics challenge us to look at the consequences when toleration is absent. But toleration is laden with all kinds of quagmires. Theoretically, toleration demands absolutes. Whose beliefs and values, after all, can be used to end practices that other groups consider appropriate? It would appear that any violation of the beliefs and values of other peoples is a violation of toleration. On the other hand, even toleration is a violation of the beliefs of many peoples. Indeed, for many peoples many things simply cannot be tolerated. To do so constitutes a moral and spiritual violation. As such, toleration puts a tremendous strain on our belief and value systems. It even undermines the integrity of beliefs and values of various groups by demanding such groups temper convictions to various beliefs and values. Still, proponents of race, gender and so forth tell us that this kind of burdening is necessary for the making of a good society. All that is supposedly being demanded of us is also being equally demanded of others. In a multicultural society,

Diversity

toleration is simply (and supposedly) the best that can be had.

Toleration legitimizes the status quo by religitimizing various assumptions that the status quo thrives on. It explicitly maintains the assumption that human beings have a proclivity for chaos and devolution. Toleration does this by assuming that getting along with each other is difficult. Supposedly, the best that human beings can do is to respect each other's differences. Even the most fervent proponents of toleration admit that it is a tenuous framework fraught with all kinds of contradictions, tensions, and problems. It is supposedly a matter of toleration simply being a lesser evil than assimilation. Toleration is supposedly the best that can be had. No one even takes seriously the possibility that a solution rich in beauty and symmetry is within our potentiality. Toleration turns us away from each other and towards institutions, structures, and laws. It heightens our dependency on such mechanisms. We supposedly have no natural capacity to peacefully coexist. In this way, toleration sustains a view of human beings that undermines hope and serves the ends of the status quo.

Toleration also trivializes and depoliticizes our understanding of diversity. Supposedly, diversity is about differences, differences that need to be managed. Diversity is reduced to plurality. This view of diversity poses no threat to our own ways of experiencing and being in the world. It demands no risking of life. Toleration undercuts evolution. It undercuts the evolution of new ways of experiencing and being in the world. Toleration aims to end chaos, disruption, conflict, and transgression. Its goal is stability and order. However, in seeking to end chaos and other such forces, toleration disrupts the natural order and rhythm of the world. In fact, in seeking to end chaos, disruption, conflict, and transgression, toleration undermines the potentiality and well-being of the world. In other words, there is no fundamental difference in the ambition of both assimilation and toleration politics. Both focus on managing our differences so as to save us from our supposedly malevolent proclivity.

Diversity As A Verb

Diversity forces us to develop new ways of being and experiencing the world. It is about depriviling worldviews and delegitimizing relations of power that control and suppress other ways of being and understandings of the world. Diversity contests the legitimacy of the status quo. Most of all, like forest fires, diversity heightens the vitality of natural systems, like human systems. Diversity is a catalyst. To look at diversity in the way I am describing verbs our understanding of diversity. Diversity is a natural occurring phenomenon found in all natural systems. It transcends race, ethnicity, sexual orientation, and other such differences. *Diversity is any new and different way of being and experiencing the world that fosters growth and development of systems and collectives.* To look at diversity in terms of ethnicity, race, and so forth misses the diversity potentiality that resides within supposedly homogeneous groups of race, ethnicity, and so forth. It also misses the chaos, disruption, and conflict that exist within supposedly homogeneous groups. In doing so, it overly exaggerates the level of homogeneity and stability that such groups reflect and claim. Further, this view of diversity misses the reality that all groups—regardless of race, ethnicity, and so forth—must harness the virtues of diversity. In other words, a verb understanding of diversity gives diversity a moral foundation.

Diversity

I do not claim any ability to read God's mind. I am sure of only one thing. When we look at the glory of stars and galaxies in the sky and the glory of forests and flowers in the living world around us, it is evident that God loves diversity. Perhaps the universe is constructed according to a principle of maximum diversity. The principle of maximum diversity says that the laws of nature, and the initial conditions at the beginning of time, are such as to make the universe as interesting as possible. As a result, life is possible but not too easy.

Freeman Dyson, Nobel Laureate

A verb understanding of diversity exposes race, ethnicity, and so forth as purely social constructs. It also exposes how theoretically and morally bankrupt is our common definition of diversity. Our humanity transcends our race, ethnicity, sexual orientation, and other such differences. Diversity is a phenomenon that belongs to the world. It reveals to us a lot about the nature of the world. It also tells us a lot about the potentiality of the world. Diversity reveals a world laden with beauty and potentiality. It also reveals a moral world. Actions that thwart the evolution of systems thwart life. Further, actions that aim to end conflict, chaos, and so forth thwart life. Diversity celebrates the present and the future. It has no binding obligation to the past.

Being beholden to our race, ethnicity, sexual orientation, and so forth is a violation of the natural order and rhythm of the world. This is how a politics that is based on differences harms us. Such a politics blocks us from transcending our differences. In doing so, such a politics blocks our evolution and transformation. That is, such a politics blocks our becoming fully human by thwarting the evolution of our potentiality. Such a politics ultimately reduces us to beasts. On the other hand, the sum of our humanity is by no means determined by our differences. Our differences are only a reflection of the richness of the world. Behind our differences is a common potentiality. We are all of this potentiality. This potentiality bounds and shapes us. We are—regardless of our differences—obligated to foster ways of being that promote evolution.

Any politics that is committed to diversity must be committed to evolution. That is, such a politics must be committed to us becoming fully human. It must also be committed to ending hierarchy and the devolution of rigid and complex structures and institutions. Both arrangements block disequilibrium, chaos, conflict, and disruption. What is required is a commitment to deepen our cognitive, sensual, and spiritual capacity so as to strengthen our ability to better deal with the ambiguity of the world. In turn, this requires a commitment to relations that exercise trust, compassion, cooperation, and openness. This is the only kind of relations that exercises and expands our humanity. In this way, diversity is about relations that allow for the communion of differences. Communion is about the deepening of our humanity through relations that foster union rather than fragmentation. It accents our moral, existential, and spiritual strives for union with the world and each other.

Diversity as a noun versus diversity as a verb represents different worldviews. The latter calls for a paradigm shift— new understandings of the world, each other, and what being human means. The different worldviews make and reflect different ways of being and experiencing the world. Diversity as a noun assumes a bifurcation between us and the world. It also assumes that the world is in conflict with us. Supposedly, our survival and well being are dependent on us controlling and predicting and manipulating the forces of the world through the development of sophisticated techniques, methods, and machines. The assumption being that human beings have the ability to control, predict, and manipulate the forces of the world. This notion that human beings and the world are in conflict with each other makes for a deep distrust and suspicion of the world.

Diversity, Time & Space

Diversity as a noun strives on causation. It assumes that our race, gender, and other differences causally affect our ways of being in the world. It is for this reason that diversity as a noun is fixated with reifying and perpetuating a politics of differences. It assumes that the end of differences would mean an end to diversity, or the different behaviors that supposedly flow from our differences. On the other hand, causation presumably gives us the ability to order and control a world that is supposedly in conflict with us. We are therefore determined to know how our differences affect our ways of being in the world. We are also equally determined to use such supposed truths to order and control our society through the politics of division and fragmentation. The result is an ideology that permeates our consciousness with all kinds of ugly stereotypes.

Causation fixates us on the physical and material realm of the world. It strives to strip away all of the complexity and ambiguity that constitute the world. It emasculates all of the complex relationships that constitute the world. It deterministically reduces all of the world to relations of causes and effects. This ambition to deconstruct the world reduces the world to a physical phenomenon. We expect to physically identify all causes and effects. We expect to understand completely. This emphasis on physicality now permeates our consciousness of the world.

Literality Promotes Homogeneity

We have reduced human beings to different physical features, such as race, ethnicity, gender and so forth. We have reduced diversity to differences. We have reduced communication to symbols and signs and messages. Physicality translates to a focus on the material and, in so doing, a downplaying of the existential and spiritual dimensions of the world. What ultimately evolves is us acting and experiencing the world literally. Literal peoples aim to attach experiences to signs and symbols and codes. This is the only way our experiences and truths attain currency. Conversely, such peoples expect signs and symbols and codes to capture all that makes us human.

Literal peoples generally aim to experience the world efficiently rather than deeply. The goal is to control our experiencing of the world by controlling our relation to the world and other human beings. This is partially accomplished through an overly heavy dependency on signs, symbols, and codes. Literal peoples also generally have a high sensibility to language use. Supposedly, meaning resides within symbols, signs, and codes. This way of placing meaning allows us to control and limit our experiencing of the world. Meanings and experiences that fall outside of our codes, symbols, and signs are simply pushed away from our consciousness. No doubt the meanings and experiences that will tend to do so would have the most passion and intensity. In this way, locating meanings in symbols, codes, and signs limit any deep exploration of the human condition.

Literality controls and limits our experiencing of the world. It is naturally hostile to nonlinear experiences and motives. It subtly forces us to act and experience the world linearly, causally, and rationally. Literality disciplines us. It is institutional, that is, rigidly structured. Focus is on the written rather than the spoken word. In fact, the written word is privileged. Focus is also on documenting and recording our experiences. We want our languages and symbols to accurately mirror the world and perfectly capture our experiences. We stress reproduction rather than interpretation. As with any institution, the goal is stability and homogeneity. This is achieved through the suppression of new experiences that can possibly threaten the status quo. Institutions and rigid structures block spontaneity, diversity, evolution, and transformation. What results is a fixed reality. That is, rather than enabling new and different ways of experiencing the world, literality sustains the status quo.

Literality fosters a deep fear of the world by assuming that institutionalization of language is vital for the evolution of the good society. As such, literal peoples generally tend to reduce communication to language. This always happens when relationships are deemphasized. The reason being that communication is fundamentally a relational phenomenon. Relationships are created, negotiated, and sustained through communication. Consequently, when communication is deemphasized, relationships are also deemphasized. What emerges are redundant systems of institutions, structures, and laws. The redundancy of such systems is the hallmark of literal peoples.

Literal peoples also generally have a deep distrust of diversity, and naturally so. Diversity is seen as a threat to the stability and order that they are aspiring to achieve. Moreover, such peoples lack the temperament and techniques to deal with diversity. Diversity demands systems that are open to new and different ways of experiencing the world. It requires systems that ebb and flow to the natural quantum rhythms of the world. Diversity also demands the opportunity for interpretation and reinterpretation. In short, diversity demands communication rather than language. Unfortunately, however, identity politics emphasizes language by promoting speech codes, gender neutral language, and other linguistic practices that do nothing to lessen the threat of our differences that result from us being estranged from each other. In fact, these practices actually promote separation by undermining the honest, open, and robust (even loud) exchanges that are so vital to us understanding each other.

Communication precedes and transcends language. It is inherently ontological. In other words, communication is about us being in the world. Language is an artifact of communication. That is, communication is by no means dependent on language. Newborns and toddlers show us this again and again. It is only communication that sustains the human condition, which is to say that communication constitutes us. As communication precedes and transcends language, meanings also transcend signs, symbols, and codes. We do acquire meanings about the world and ourselves outside of language, symbols, and codes. It is our natural questing for meaning that pushes and bends and exceeds our symbols, signs, and codes. Communication shapes language use. It is for this reason that even against our most strenuous efforts, our languages are always changing and evolving. Thus attempts to hold our language constant and undercut the evolution of communication are violations against the human condition. Literality undercuts the expansion of our humanity by blocking the natural rhythms of evolution that are vital for achieving deeper and richer experiences of the world and each other. In so doing, literality makes us less human.

Literality extricates language from communication.

Diversity

Language becomes synonymous with communication. In fact, language becomes communication. No communication can supposedly occur without language. We assume therefore that communication requires a common set of codes and symbols. The corollary of this is that communication requires a common set of experiences and worldviews. Supposedly, without us possessing a common set of codes, symbols, and signals, communication is impossible. So we insist on the need of having a common language so as to get along productively and peacefully. We also stress language competency and the need to build our vocabulary so to better express ourselves.

Literality reduces communication competency to skills and techniques. It reduces communication to an artifact of being. It assumes no constitutive function of communication in being human. Literality therefore takes the passion, complexity, and mystery out of communication. It also takes meanings and relationships out of communication. In other words, literality takes the human component out of communication. Yet this is exactly the ambition of literality: to demystify and simplify the world, to reduce the world to a set of linear and causal relations so as to better predict and control the supposedly malevolent forces of the world that are in conflict with us. To this end, language becomes an instrument, requiring all the precision and skills that good instruments demand.

We stress good language use and clarity of expression. We assume that we have the ability to perfectly and completely control the expression of our thoughts and feelings. Supposedly, communication is about packaging, transmitting, and interpreting messages. We also assume that the goal of completely and perfectly controlling the expression of out thoughts and feelings is a good thing. Of course vital to doing so is our ability to use language precisely and competently. We therefore stress exercises that will expand our language competency.

But in no way do we have the ability or potentiality to completely and perfectly control the expression of our thoughts and feelings and nothing about trying to do this serves us well. Our striving for meaning precedes and exceeds us. We are always negotiating meaning. Meaning permeates our being, our relations to the world and each other. We are no doubt *languaged* beings. However, communication exceeds and precedes language. Language only facilitates communication. It is our striving for meaning that situates us always within relations to ourselves, each other, and the world. Communication embeds us within the world and each other. We ebb and flow to the rhythms of the world through communication. The rhythms of the world are constantly tugging and pushing and bending us. To be embedded in the world is to be entwined within the world. In extricating the human component from communication, as well as extricating language from communication, literality extricates—really rips—us from the world. It makes for the illusion that the world is outside of us, separate from us, different from us, beyond us. Language becomes instrumental and mechanical—that is, devoid of passion and rhythm. Focus is on the written word.

Literality displaces orality. Oral traditions and practices are lost. We no longer embody the world as narrative beings. Our story telling capacity is lost. We no longer construct our understandings of the world through tales and narratives. Our narratives and tales no longer connect and bound us. Literality displaces us. It disconnects us. It lessens our connectedness to each other. However, orality best positions us to ebb and flow with the rhythms of the world. Orality places us in the center at the cosmos. A life-world built around narratives is one built upon meaning and interpretation. Each telling and retelling of a story makes for new meanings and interpretations. It is through this telling and retelling we bend and move to the natural rhythms of the world. Narratives organically exercise us. New meanings give us new and different ways of experiencing the world. In this way, oral traditions undercut the formation of rigid structures and institutions.

Diversity as a verb also operates on a different assumption of space. Diversity as a noun is drawn from a worldview that uses space to maintain order and control. Focus is on division and separation so as to limit the pollution and assimilation of our differences. Focus is also on the creation of spaces for different groups. Supposedly, the hallmark of a good society is one that creates and respects the spaces of different groups. Diversity as a noun is of a worldview that maintains well-organized spaces. Spaces are rigidly defined and controlled. We also find an elaboration of space so as to increase the physical separation between and among groups. We find physical and material points of demarcation so as to identify what spaces belong to which groups. A lot of attention is devoted to maintaining such points of demarcation. Increasingly, such points are becoming literally physical. We use high fences and all kinds of rigid walls. Our spaces turn us inward rather than outward. Walls are ubiquitous. Our control of space is really about our need to limit and control movements and contact. We fear that the lack of this kind of control will bring chaos and devolution. We use space to help us control and order the world, and, as always, such control begins with our own control of our humanity and our control of others. We expect our spaces to maintain the differences that are supposedly natural of this world.

Hierarchy is a creation of our dominant understanding of time and space. Its creation is born out of our ambition to control and order the forces of the world. Hierarchy assumes that human beings can be controlled through the manipulation of various factors. Its goal is to identify what causes make for what effects. It assumes, for example, that our race, gender, sexual orientation, and so forth make for certain kinds of behaviors. It ultimately believes that human action is controlled by either forces of sociology, psychology, or biology.

We now have a full industry devoted to identifying genes with different behaviors. We want to know what persons have what genes. Our goal is no doubt to attain maximum control. We want to end all ambiguity that comes with being human. Yet we seem to have no problem reducing our humanity to our biology. Indeed, discussions of social class are no longer stigmatized. We are increasingly and openly and unapolegitically discussing how biology affects human behaviors. Proponents of biology contend that identity politics is yet to give us viable and reasonable alternatives to the status quo. Presumably, identity politics is yet to deal honestly and competently with supposedly many *hard* truths, such as the supposed superiority of different races, the supposed natural differences between men and women that make for patriarchy, and the supposed fact that hierarchy is the order of the world.

We are increasingly treating human beings as, to use Richard Dawkins' language, "survival machines"—mechanisms created to do the selfish bidding of our genes for purely purposes of survival. Increasingly, this is what prominent and distinguished scientists posit: human beings have no natural moral, existential, or spiritual capacity or potentiality. We are supposedly merely bundles of genes who are battling to survive and evolve. As such, national policy is increasingly being shaped by the view that human beings are fundamentally biological beings.

Diversity

It rapidly became clear to me that the most imaginative way of looking at evolution, and the most inspiring way of teaching it, was to say that it's all about the genes. It's the genes that, for their own good, are manipulating the bodies they ride about in. The individual organism is a survival machine for its genes. . . .

Nature really is red in tooth and claw. Much as we might like to believe otherwise, natural selection, working within each species, does not favor long-term stewardship. It favors short-term gain. Loggers, whalers, and other profiteers who squander the future for present greed, are only doing what all wild creatures have done for three billion years.

Richard Dawkins, Charles Simonyi Professor For Understanding Of Science, Oxford University

But biology makes no demands on us. Its simplicity is appealing. It gives us nice and easy explanations of human behavior. Biology works as both an explanation and a justification. It rationalizes our unwillingness to risk life so as to expand our humanity. It also rationalizes all the behaviors and practices that come with being less human. That is, it legitimizes all the behaviors and practices that give legitimacy to the status quo. It reinforces the notion that human beings are beasts.

Biology plays well with a society that celebrates competition. It assumes that the status quo gives us the opportunity to get our just regards. It is simply a matter of getting up and get. Thus ever so often the status quo will point to the material success of persons of historically and marginalized groups as proof that the status quo offers equal opportunity for material success. This fixation on opportunity and material success works to downplay any belief that human beings are also existential and spiritual beings. Any politics that rests on this belief is suppressed.

On the other hand, western civilization has long been determined to attain perfect control and order over this world. We have sequestered medical, social, technical, and mechanical technology to attain this goal. This goal is the impetus behind our current technology revolution.

We look at the evolution of modern technology as progress. Supposedly, this evolution reflects our increasing ability to control and harness the forces of the world. We determine the success of any new technology by its ability to help us command the forces of the world. We now aim for technology to end the supposed tyranny of ethnicity, geography, and language. We want a world that diminishes such differences, or at least those differences that impede the evolution of global capitalism. Supposedly, such differences undercut global development, that is, the development that comes supposedly with the evolution of the world. We profess to want a world without structures that hinder access and penetration. Thus, behind the evolution of technology is the belief that human beings and the world are in conflict with each other and, moreover, that the world possesses a proclivity for chaos and devolution. Modern technology assumes a power to control and order.

It would appear that technology is giving us the power to control and order the forces of the world. We consistently hear of new technology breakthroughs. It does seem that technology is giving us the power and the upper hand in our supposed conflict with the world. We appear to be winning the war with the natural world. We increasingly hear that remaining battles will soon be won as soon as the technology becomes available. It is apparently only a matter of time before victory is ours. Technology will supposedly release us from the ambiguity of the world. We are increasingly preaching this gospel to supposedly developing nations. Technology will end hunger, poverty, and other kinds of human misery. Its promises are no doubt tempting, especially for peoples who must confront the full brunt of human misery. However, missed with this sell is the fact that this technology—with its causation ethos—also brings a worldview that changes our relations to the world and each other.

Our worldview is contrary to that of many peoples. Many worldviews posit no conflict between the world and us. Neither do many cultures posit that human beings have the ability to control and order the forces of the world. In sum, many peoples have no grand ambition to control and order the world. The nature of the world is taken as a given. The world is seen spiritually rather than mechanically. In other words, modern technology reflects a pernicious form of colonialism. It subtly changes our relations to the world, each other, and our own humanity. It homogenizes us. It also moves us towards an overly muscular orientation to the world. We need only look at how medical technology boasts of waging wars upon various diseases, of finding the new ammunition—"the new bullets"—that will allow us to conquer deadly diseases. We focus on control rather than on harmony. We are no longer willing to accept any ambiguity and disequilibrium that come with the world. We are now committed to ending both. Herein resides the problem with modern technology and the threat that it poses to the world.

I think it is no exaggeration to say we are on the cusp of the further perfection of extreme evil, an evil whose possibility spreads well beyond that which weapons of mass destruction bequeathed to the nation-states, on to a surprising and terrible empowerment of extreme individuals. . . . We are being propelled into this new century with no plan, no control, no brakes. Have we already gone too far down the path to alter course? I don't believe so, but we

aren't trying yet, and the last change to assert control - the fail-safe point - is rapidly approaching.... Clearly, we need to find meaningful challenged and sufficient scope in our lives if we are to be happy in whatever is to come. But I believe we must find alternative outlets for our creative forces, beyond the culture of perpetual economic growth; this growth has largely been a blessing for several hundred years, but it has not brought us unalloyed happiness, and we must now choose between the pursuit of unrestricted and undirected growth through science and technology and the clear accompanying dangers.
Bill Joy, Chief Scientist
Sun Microsystem

The world is of chaos, diversity, disruption, disequilibrium, and ambiguity. No technology will ever end such forces. We have already discussed the fact that such forces are vital to the evolution and well being of the world. Yet this remains the mission of our technology: to end ambiguity and disequilibrium. In aiming to end all mystery and ambiguity so as to give us the ability to control and order the world, we are now perilously threatening to end the world. Modern technology is antagonizing and destabilizing the natural opposing forces of the world. We are increasingly pushing up against the limits of the world.

The newfound power that our technology is amassing is reinforcing our belief that we have the potential to command the world. We assume that it is merely a matter of developing the proper technology and techniques. This is all that matters. We are becoming arrogant and reckless. We are overly exaggerating the promise of technology and downplaying the perils that are increasingly appearing. We are no doubt convinced that new technology would soon evolve to stop the emerging dangers. Such is our ever deepening faith in technology. Technology can supposedly do no wrong. The

Diversity

problem is always with the kind of technology or the maturity of the technology. We will never question the mission of technology or the worldview that is shaping and driving the evolution of much of modern technology. Technology will never give us the ability to completely order and control the world. We can obviously try, but such an ability was never given to us. The world simply disallows the full playing out of such an ambition. We are, like all the other life forms found in this world, of the world. We are embedded within the world. We are therefore of the complexity, nonlinearity, diversity, mystery, and ambiguity that constitute the world. It is all of this that makes us human and sustains our humanity. To end any of this is to end our humanity.

VI
The New Politics

There is no organizing principle by which you could put 5 billion people into so few [racial] categories in a way that would tell you anything important about humankind's diversity.
C. Loring Brace, Michigan University

While biological traits give the impression that race is a biological unit of nature. It remains a cultural construct. The boundaries between races depends on the classifier's own cultural norms.
George Armelagos, Emory University

The obsession with broad [racial] categories is so powerful as to seem a neurological imperative. Changing our thinking about race will require a revolution in thought as profound, and profoundly unsettling, as anything science has ever demanded. What these researchers are talking about is changing the way in which we see the world and each other. But before that can happen, we must do more than understand the biologist's suspicions about race. We must ask science, also, why it is that we are so intent on sorting humanity into so few groups—us and Other—In the first place.

Sharon Begley, Newsweek

Diversity

The status quo needs to reify our differences. It needs us to focus on our differences rather than our common humanness and humanity. It needs us to view our differences as natural and real and binding. To focus on our common humanity makes for a moral and political obligation to provide equally for all. This obligation would naturally demand a redistribution of wealth and resources. It would undercut hierarchy. It would also undercut apathy and selfishness. Focusing on our common humanness would expand our humanity so to accept our differences, but yet also push us beyond the fear and anxiety that come with our differences so as to reach and affirm our common humanity. Such a focus would deepen our compassion, regardless of how different our differences. But all of this would threaten the status quo. So, the status quo needs differences. We need differences. We need ready and easy excuses to justify our unwillingness to confront the ambiguity of the world. We need an excuse to justify our fear to risk life, the kind of risking that expands our humanity. We need an excuse to justify our deepest fears of the world. We need excuses to avoid the suffering that comes with learning new ways of being and experiencing the world.

But identity is a complex phenomenon. It is difficult to surrender our differences. Our differences come with different burdens—burdens of bigotry, persecution, discrimination, and survival. Identity also often comes with privileges and rewards. Identity never appears in a historical vacuum. It is as much social as historical. Calls to unilaterally disarm ourselves of our differences show no deep understanding of what identity is about. No identity is ever apolitical, asocial, and acultural. This is a myth that the politics of class perpetuates. The problems that confront us have nothing to do with our differences. Our problems begin and end with separation.

Identity politics forces different groups to bear the burdens of identity separately. This practice perpetuates the illusion that our burdens are different. It also assumes that the origins of our burdens are different. Identity politics fragments us. We all attend to our own burdens, developing in the process a commitment to protect our own identity. Identity becomes like a god, demanding our full submission. To abandon our identity of differences is to face rejection and isolation. We are seen as rejecting our responsibility to help carry the burdens that come with our differences. We are also seen as disrespecting the sufferings and sacrifices of our ancestors. In both ways, identity politics subtly bounds us to an identity that is shaped out of our differences. We are always fundamentally defined in terms of our race, ethnicity, sexual orientation, and gender. Efforts to define us differently are fraught with peril.

It hurts us when different groups bear the burdens of identity separately. This practice perpetuates fragmentation rather than union. The reason being that, regardless of our differences, all our burdens have origins in us being less human. We are all victims. We are all conspirators in the creation of other's burdens. Identity is always created through the forces of oppression and liberation. Identity is dialectical. We all have a moral responsibility to help each other carry the burdens of others as doing so will help us expand our humanity. It will also foreground our responsibility in the suffering of others. All of this will bear negatively on the status quo. We will be forced to develop a politics that enlarges our commitment to each other.

An identity that is shaped and bound to differences is also a limited identity. This kind of identity undercuts the expansion of our humanity. It undercuts our exercising of love and compassion. It makes for a politics bent on keeping our identity constant. But such an identity keeps us beholden to a set way of viewing, experiencing, and being in the world. Such an identity bounds us the past by making us afraid of the natural quantum rhythms of the world that push to transcend the present. Our identity becomes a marker, a means of showing our affiliation and membership. But no identity should demand this kind of loyalty. It is even perilous—from a system standpoint—to hold to a conception of identity that is beholden to the past. The world demands constant construction and reconstruction of our identity. Our identity needs to serve us rather than us serve our identity. Human beings quest for meaning creation. We are constantly questing for new ways of being and experiencing the world. A new identity means a new way of experiencing and being in the world. It means a deepening of our humanity. The notion that identity is constant or can remain constant is an illusion. Our questing for meaning is always pushing up against our identity. Our identity is always evolving and changing.

To ground our identity in our race, gender, nationality, and so forth is to limit our identity to a worldview that is obsessed with differences. Our identity needs to allow for new ways of understanding and experiencing the world. This will mean an identity that allows us to move beyond what is presumed to be our common differences. This will also mean an identity that releases us from the past. We are, again, *culturing* beings. We are always creating new and different cultures.

Identity & Meaning

Our quest for meaning is fundamentally a relational

phenomenon. It occurs between us and the world, us and each other, and between our humanity and us. Human beings are fundamentally relational beings. We find our humanity through each other. Identity shows us belonging to a set of relationships. At the deepest level, identity reflects our search for community, our need to belong, our need to avoid isolation. On the other hand, human beings strive for deep and complex relations. It is this deepening that destabilizes our identity. Deepening any relationships expands our humanity. It moves us beyond our differences.

So any identity that is fundamentally based on our differences fosters fragmentation rather than union. Such an identity makes us less human by undercutting our own natural striving for evolution and transformation. In so doing, such an identity blocks us from transcending our differences, thereby allowing us to move to an identity that foregrounds our common humanity. Evolution and transformation are the pathways to union. To become fully human is to gain the ability to look beyond our differences to our common humanity with others. It is about coming to a deep understanding of the relation between diversity and union.

Identity can never be held constant. The reason again being that identity was never meant to be held constant. The forces of the world verb identity. When left to the rhythms of the world, identity will bend and fold. We can do nothing to stop this reality. But nothing is yet to stop us from trying. But at what cost? That is, what is the cost to trying to hold identity constant? History reveals a hell of a cost. Wars upon wars have been fought over either extending or defending all kinds of identity. We are still soaking a lot of land with a lot of blood over identity. Identity wars appear to have no end in sight.

The identity that emerges out of the politics of both class

and differences mystify us. We mystify ourselves so as to justify our supposed separation from the world and each other. This justification is based on fabrications, distortions, and illusions. We mystify so as to deny, defend, and excuse. Mystification exaggerates our differences. It allows us to deny our own striving for union. It allows us to pacify the anxiety that attend to separation. Mystification limits human action. It gives us a way to justify our unwillingness to risk life. It gives us ready excuses and ready rationales for actions and lack thereof. That is, mystification maintains our separation. This separation evolves to a separation from our humanity to each other and the world. Eventually, mystification extends to our relations with others and the world. We find the evolution of a worldview that is based on superstition and mysticism. Our illusions, distortions, and fabrications of each other are aptly seen in our creation of all kinds of arbitrary differences and the various stereotypes that attend to different groups.

We know that race is an illusion. We know that IQ is an illusion. We also know that the growing disparity in the distribution of wealth has nothing to do with biology. Yet these kinds of fabrications have evolved to justify separation and thereby maintain the fiction that our humanity is different. The result being an identity of ourselves that is based on fabrications, fictions, and illusions. Our illusions, fabrications, and distortions of the world are many. All posit a separation between the world and us. Yet no such separation exists. We also posit a world that is divided between matter and forces. But no such separation exists. We also posit a world that is fixed. Yet this is an evolving and emerging world. It is fluid rather than rigid. We also know that our deep distrust and suspicion of the world is without ground. The world is in no way in conflict with us. We also know that our deep distrust and suspicion of our humanity is without ground.

Final Thoughts

Our extant relation to others, the world, and our own identity—the relations that collectively shape our humanity—are based on illusions, fabrications, and distortions so as to justify separation. So our identity must constantly be propped up, always requiring new and grander illusions, fabrications, and distortions. It is an obligation that naturally consumes us as so much energy is required to find new illusions, fabrications, and distortions. Still, this kind of identity is existentially vacuous. It debilitates the human condition. This debilitation is aptly seen in the increasing rise of mental sickness and human misery. This kind of identity alienates us from our humanity. On the other hand, our dependency on new and grander illusions, fabrications, and distortions only fosters and deepens separation, and conversely pushes us further and further away from union. But there is only so much fragmentation, separation, and alienation that the human condition that withstand. We are obviously now perilously approaching this point.

What is further damning is the fact that this deepening fragmentation and separation is kept up by us positing a deep suspicion and distrust of each other, the world, and our humanity. This distrust and suspicion is also vital to legitimizing our new found separation and fragmentation. What is evolving is an identity that is increasingly shaped in distrust and suspicion, an identity that is increasingly in conflict with itself. This kind of identity is fostering a politics that actually celebrates distrust and suspicion. This politics is increasingly replacing identity politics. It is a new politics of class. In this new class politics, identity is foremost shaped and determined by self-interests rather than by group affiliation. It is assumed that human beings have no moral, existential, and spiritual obligation to each other. Supposedly, self-interest is the soul of human existence. This new politics of class views each human being as a competitor that is always scheming, conniving, and fighting for limited resources. Identity is about status, our position on the hierarchical food chain.

VII

Communion

Nobody is against diversity. Most peoples generally agree that diversity is good and should even be encouraged. With identity politics, what concerns us are such questions like, how much diversity is necessary, what kind of diversity is good, who decides how much and what kinds of diversity, and when is diversity good versus when is diversity bad. We generally assume that without proper mechanisms any society can possibly have too much diversity or even foster the wrong kinds of diversity. As such, the focus is on diversity management. We also view diversity functionally—diversity affords superior decision-making, promotes creativity, expands access to new markets and resources, and so forth. We look at diversity as a means to an end. It presumably enhances the performing of different functions.

Diversity training programs and initiatives focus on harnessing the potential of diversity. Diversity is seen as a commodity that comes with the addition of peoples of different races, gender, ethnicity, and so forth. Any collective can supposedly become diverse through the process of addition. Recognizing the many virtues that diversity brings, many collectives are now committed to adding all kinds of differences. Persons of historically marginalized and disenfranchised groups are now being vigorously pursued—always strongly encouraged to apply. We all now want our own minority. Economically, times have never been better for members of marginalized and disenfranchised groups—at least this is what the status quo tells us again and again.

Diversity

Identity politics warns us about the emerging threats to our progress and prosperity, about the assaults upon various programs that have supposedly propelled us forward and onward, and about our responsibility to push ahead so as to tear down the remaining walls that block our full access to wealth and power. In this case, diversity is about opportunity and proportionality. Diversity is supposedly achieved when members of historically marginalized and disenfranchised groups attain fair opportunity and proportionality. In the end, all sides cast diversity in terms of economics, politics, and profits.

The point I have sought to make throughout this book is that our dominant understanding of diversity poses no threat to the status quo. We are working with a shallow understanding of diversity. The status quo actually profits when diversity is cast in terms of economics and politics. Diversity as differences reduces diversity to a commodity, and any commodity can be purchased. Moreover, diversity as differences relegitimizes bedrock assumptions of the world and our own humanity that the status quo uses to limit and suppress human action, thereby undercutting the possibility of new ways of being and experiencing the world. Identity politics aides and abets the status quo by viewing diversity as a goal that the status quo is morally obligated to meet. The fact is, as our society pushes towards this goal, the gap between rich and poor grows exponentially, human despair and misery is reaching newfound levels, and the environment appears to be collapsing from our unrelenting plunder. Diversity as a goal promises no end to such emerging truths that now perilously threaten to destroy both the world and our own humanity. We need, besides a new understanding of diversity, as well as a new politics, a new goal. I contend that this goal should be communion.

We have no need to worry about the end of diversity.

Communion will organically bring forth all the diversity that the potentiality of the world offers. Diversity is an artifact of communion. Its evolution reflects the forging of union and, by that, the lessening of our distrust and suspicion of each other. Communion as a goal reminds us that the task of liberation begins at the level of worldview. We need new understandings and relations to the world, each other, and our own humanity. We need revolution rather than reform. We need a worldview that foregrounds notions like union and potentiality. Only such a worldview can give us the mechanisms to foster new and different ways of being and experiencing the world that will make for the evolution and expansion of our humanity. We need a worldview that fosters hope and goodwill rather than distrust and suspicion. To look at diversity at the level of worldview reveals that we have a lot of work to do. Stripping ourselves of a worldview is difficult. Worldviews are pernicious. All of our hopes and fears belong to worldviews. Discarding our assumptions, beliefs, and truths demand much less risking of life than surrendering our hopes and fears. Our hopes and fears exercise a tremendous amount of control on our lives.

To abandon a worldview calls forth a willingness to risk life. No new worldview emerges without such a commitment. Communion as a goal makes this plain to us. No revolution comes without a price, without sacrifices, without suffering. Yet all revolutions are local. All revolutions begin and end with each person, each relationship, each collective forging the evolution of new ways of being and experiencing the world. To look at the matter at the level of worldview therefore focuses us on the need to transform our relations to each other, each other, and our own humanity so as to get beyond the status quo. Union must be forged in each relation.

Communion gives us a deep moral understanding of the

world and what being human means. Communion obligates us to foster ways of being that expand our humanity. We are to foster revolution and transformation so as to afford new and different ways of being experiencing the world. We are to foster trust, compassion, and affirmation. Communion reveals to us that our primary responsibility as human beings is to become fully human.

On Inclusion and Exclusion

The controversy over gay marriages shows the limits of our toleration of differences. Most persons who have gay friends, gay family members, gay associates, and even profess to be against discrimination against homosexuals, are staunchly against gay marriages and support legislation that will maintain the status quo. Opponents of gay marriages speak about the sanctity of marriage. On the other hand, opponents of legislation that bar gay marriages contend that such legislation is inherently discriminatory. It takes away privileges from homosexual couples that are given to heterosexual couples. Opponents vow to end such legislation. The fight is cast in terms of equality and diversity, as the new civil rights movement. Homosexuals want inclusion. Opponents of legislation that bar gay marriages are determined to expose the hypocrisy that is behind the opposition of gay marriages. Casting the matter in terms of civil rights shows how deeply it is understood within identity politics as a matter of discrimination and inclusion. Opponents of gay marriages, like proponents of gender and racial equality, are determined to end such exclusion and discrimination. For many homosexuals, marriage is the crowning achievement of inclusion and equality.

There is no doubt that homosexuals—like women and blacks—will eventually attain full inclusion. Opposition to gay marriages will eventually fall away. In the near future most of us will be attending gay marriages. History reveals that attitudes change. Marriage as an institution has always changed. We even appear to forget that until recently interracial marriages were also illegal. But gay marriages pose no threat to the status quo. The opposition to gay marriages by persons who profess to be against discrimination against gays only shows how identity politics cultivates a morally bankrupt notion of diversity.

To cast gay marriages in language of inclusion and equality is to miss an important opportunity to interrogate the status quo and to consider other ways of being and experiencing the world. The sanctioning of gay marriages will have absolutely no effect on the widening gap between rich and poor, the increasing rise of human despair and misery, the unrelenting plunder of the world's natural resources, and other manifestations of human suffering. Such marriages, in other words, will have no bearing on the condition of the world. In this way, the status quo actually wants homosexual issues to be cast in terms of exclusion and inclusion as this approach subtly controls how such issues will be resolved, and resolved in such a way that poses no threat to the status quo. On the other hand, however, the status quo is us. We all want, homosexuals and heterosexuals, gay marriages to be cast in terms of inclusion and exclusion. Ultimately, to cast the matter this way challenges us to risk no life. No new worldview is required. We are released of having to develop new ways of being and experiencing the world. We also neither have to discard our discriminatory beliefs, values, truths, assumptions, fears, and hopes that subtly harm others. To accept gay marriages merely demands a changing of attitudes. It demands no coming to terms with the human despair that increasingly pervades our being or no reckoning with the depletion of the world's natural resources. Gay marriages is supposedly and purely a homosexual matter, purely a matter of legal discrimination.

We have developed a sophisticated competency in neutralizing and coopting issues that have the potential to force us to look at the world differently. We find this competency in our handling of hate crimes, gay marriages, the widening gap between rich and poor, the allocation and distribution of the world's natural resources, and so forth. We are left with the impression that these are all difference issues involving different peoples, thus requiring different solutions. We no doubt want to create this impression. After all, this impression narrowly circumscribes our responsibility to the world and each other. We merely have to limit our concerns to the matter that supposedly relates directly to our own grouping. But apparently the world can stand only so much of our disingenuousness. Increasingly, the world is forcing us to look holistically at our problems. All of our problems have a common origin. We can never end poverty without addressing our unrelenting plunder of the world's natural resources. We can also neither hope to end discrimination without addressing the growing gap between rich and poor. In short, all of our problems spring from the separation and fragmentation that result from being less human. No social problem can be fixed without addressing this matter. In other words, the solution to our problems resides in communion.

Communion as a goal forces us to look at the world holistically. We are to look at ourselves belonging to the world rather than the world belonging to us. In so doing, communion extends our responsibility to the world and each other. It moves us beyond the differences that keep us in states of separation and fragmentation. Communion focuses us on the condition of our humanity and the humanity of others. It brings us to the realization that the condition of our humanity is directly related to the humanity of others and the condition of the world. Our redemption resides in our relations to each other. Our differences merely reflect a world that is fecund. Communion realizes that our differences expand our humanity by constantly giving us new and different ways of being and experiencing the world. A world devoid of diversity is a world devoid of new expressions of our humanity. Our differences enrich the human condition and, in so doing, enrich our understanding of the world. Communion verbs our understanding of the world. It celebrates processes rather than structures, relationships rather than institutions, and communication rather than information.

We increasingly want a society that will give us the most pleasure. But pleasure does nothing much for the human condition. In most cases, only promiscuity results from pleasure. The fleeting nature of pleasure pushes us to find new and newer ways of attaining pleasure. The result is promiscuity, an orgy of meaningless and empty experiences. Pleasure is about the body. It is nothing but physical titillation. But only so much titillation the human body can respond to. Eventually, the body becomes anaesthetized, as pleasure does absolutely nothing for us. We are in the midst of playing out our fixation with pleasure. Note the exponential rise of the pleasure industry—the ever increasing search for new highs, new rushes. We are obsessed with pleasure. Note also the fallout from our obsession with pleasure, such as the rise in drug and alcohol use in our youth and the rise of mental sickness. Report after reports tell us we are increasingly lonely. Consequently, many of us are increasingly looking to new spiritual and mystical movements to fill the voids that still exist.

This emerging mystical and spiritual movement does offer moments of stability and meaning. We do obtain pauses of relief from the hostility that the status quo bombards the human condition. In fact, this movement is only succeeding by pretending to give us deep meaning. It plays particularly well on our existential and spiritual search for deep meaning. But this movement demands nothing from us. Meaning comes without cost. In most cases, this movement teaches us to look inside ourselves for meaning. We are either looking for an experience, a person, or a location. We come to this person or location or meaning through the practice of all kinds of rites and rituals. The overriding belief in this movement is that our redemption resides within us. In the end, this mystical and spiritual movement poses no threat to the status quo as it demands no risking of life. To look within ourselves for our redemption is to downplay our ability to act purposely upon the world so as to make for a new world. Looking within also downplays our responsibility to others by masking our connection to each other. Both situations make for excuses that ultimately limit our humanity. In this way, this emerging mystical and spiritual movement fosters the belief that our redemption can be had without the risking of life that is necessary to expand our humanity. In so doing, this movement contributes to the distortion of what being human means. It too perpetuates a cheap understanding of redemption.

Human beings are meaning seeking, meaning creating, and meaning negotiating beings. It is meaning—and only meaning—that makes us human. It is our questing for meaning that distinguishes us from other life forms. From a human standpoint, meaning is sacred. Communion affirms our questing for meaning. It foregrounds the notion that the condition of our humanity is related to the condition of our meanings, or the quantity and quality of our meanings. In reality, human beings quest for new meanings. We quest for deeper meanings of the world, of each other, and of our own humanity. It is through allowing our questing for meaning to blossom that human beings become fully human. Communion is about us realizing the deepest meanings—those meanings that most embed us in the world. It is about the forging of deep relations—relations laden with trust, compassion, and transparency—with the world, each other, and our own humanity. In this way, communion turns us outward. Our redemption resides within our relationships to the world, each other, and ourselves. Communion foregrounds our responsibility to each other and all others, specifically our responsibility to exercise the deepest levels of compassion and love. It also commits us to ending hierarchy and other practices that foster fragmentation. In sum, communion commits us to union, mutuality, and equality.

Many will no doubt quarrel with the claim that all human beings have a proclivity for deep meanings. Reality supposedly gives no weight to this claim. I will also confess that I make this claim with a fair amount of ambiguity. It could well be that I am too anxious to squash the dominant claim that human beings have a proclivity for chaos, destruction, and evil, or simply too angry with our apparent unwillingness to look differently at the human condition. What I do know is that child development research consistently tells us that a lot of our humanity is shaped in childhood. Our bonding experiences, or lack thereof, significantly affect the shaping of our humanity and the framing of our relations to other human beings. Other research tells us that human beings do respond to affirmation and compassion. We also know that a reciprocal tendency shapes our relations to others—trust fosters trust, affirmation fosters affirmation, and so forth. We also know that human beings have a proclivity to be transparent to the world and that the suppression of this proclivity harms us. We also know that transparency produces equality and fosters mutuality, and empathy produces equality and mutuality. We also know that less hierarchical cultures have lower levels of dysfunctionality and deviancy.

Scholars, theologians, and others who are quick to tell us about the evils of being human have a consistent tendency of never telling us about any research or observation that possibly reveals a different understanding of what being human means. Yet, the research that I just briefly noted does tell us that human beings do have a natural questing for union and through the realizing of this questing become fully human. Our striving for meaning reflects our striving for union. It is through our pursuit of deep meanings that our relations deepen, that is, move towards union. Meaning is our pathway, our catalyst, our energy, our direction, our rhythm. Meaning pulls us towards each other. What matters most is whether our meanings are allowing for as much equilibrium as disequilibrium, as much order as chaos, as much continuity as discontinuity, as much homogeneity as diversity, and so forth. Vibrant meaning creation practices expand the human condition. Our meanings must continuously make for new ways of experiencing and being in the world. Our meanings must push us outward and forward into the world, which is to say that our meanings must give us hope and faith. Our meanings must never behold us to neither the past nor the present. Our meanings must never foster fear and despair. In sum, our meanings should never limit our humanity, as reality teaches us that to do so is to foster entropy. Communion gives life deep meaning. It reveals a lot about the beauty and symmetry of the world. It tells us a lot about what being human means. Communion also reveals a lot about our relations to the world and each other. It reveals to us that human beings are moral, existential, and spiritual beings. We quest for meanings and experiences that are always beyond us yet within our grasp. We become fully human by reaching out and being selfless.

Identity politics gives us no deep meaning or moral and spiritual foundation as to why human beings are morally and spiritually obligated to end discrimination and to foster diversity. Natural systems make for a compelling case for diversity. All natural systems organically foster diversity. Such systems will perish without diversity. We already know the many virtues that diversity brings to natural systems. Indeed, natural systems make for a solid ethical and theoretical foundation for emerging understandings of diversity. But the fact is that human beings are also spiritual beings. To look at human beings within the prism of life forms who belong to natural systems, and thus obligated to move to the forces and rhythms of such systems, still distorts our understanding of what being human means. Any distortion or downplaying of all the complexity that constitutes what being human means has the possibility to make for a politics that ultimately harms the human condition. Any understanding of diversity that is devoid of a spiritual dimension has the potential to view diversity merely in terms of functionality. Our spiritual striving makes for a spiritual obligation to foster diversity, mutuality, and equality. Besides being vital to the expansion of humanity, diversity makes for communion with the world. Diversity is integral to our redemption and salvation. Simply put, communion deepens our obligation to diversity. It elevates diversity to a new paradigm. It moves diversity completely beyond the realm of functionality without downplaying the virtues that diversity brings to natural systems. Communion undercuts the cooptation of diversity. To look at diversity in terms of communion means also to look differently at what being human means, as well as to look differently at the world and each other. Communion forces us to look at diversity in terms of revolution.

The Perils Of Global Capitalism

Identity politics gives us no calculus to resist global capitalism. Global capitalism is actually bent on squashing identity politics. It aims to end what its proponents refer to as the tyranny of race, identity, nationality, ethnicity, and geography. Global capitalism is bent on homogenizing the world. Supposedly, global capitalism is progress. It will supposedly bring prosperity and development to the non-western world. It will give such peoples a proven calculus to better harness and control the resources of the world. Its structures will supposedly bring forth the good society by disciplining our ways of being in the world. Supposedly, global capitalism checks our supposed proclivity for chaos and devolution. It reflects the natural march of human evolution. The assumption being that the diversity of the world reflects backwardness. Accordingly, proponents of global capitalism mock identity politics. Proponents gloat about the supposed virtues and gains that global capitalism brings to developing nations. Supposedly, to be against global capitalism is to be against progress. Opponents are also accused of enjoying the gains of global capitalism but yet unwilling to have others also enjoy such gains. Proponents claim that peoples in developing nations overwhelmingly want global capitalism—the crowning achievement of western civilization. Indeed, many peoples in developing do seem to want capitalism.

In the last 20 years or so, and especially in the last 10,

the world has undergone a set of very different experiences, good and bad, which are bound to cast a newer light on the old questions about universal destiny. It has become obvious that, all over the world in our present age, only one kind of economic system is capable of producing significant wealth— the system of regulated markets. It has become obvious that regulated markets can prosper not just in northern Europe and North America, as many a thoughtful person had once imagine, but as far afield as America, as many a thoughtful person had once imagine, but as far afield as East Asia, which is to say, everywhere.
Paul Berman,
The Wilson Quarterly
Summer 1999

Citizens of developing countries have only one possible path out of the horrifying levels of poverty, malnutrition and disease in which the live: economic growth. And every country in history that has raised its living standards— including the United States—has done so by hitching its wagon to the world economy.
Fareed Zakaria, Newsweek
December 13, 1999

Global capitalism is no doubt on the march. It is achieving deep penetration in many different nations and cultures. Even many opponents of global capitalism admit that global capitalism does reflect the march of progress. As such, many persons now resign themselves to figuring out how best *to do* global capitalism so as to lessen its deleterious effects on different groups.

A backlash [against globalization] is certainly coming. The challenge for those of us who believe that free trade and global capital are essentially good things if managed correctly is to avoid the backlash by developing progressive

Diversity

strategies to overcome the widening inequalities and the environmental depredations while preserving what's good about globalization. And what's good about globalization needs to be on the table as well. Since the Second World War, globalization has dramatically improved the lives of most of the world's people. It has meant that poor people even in rich nations have access to goods and services that are much cheaper than they would be if we were living in a world of autarky. It means that savings can flow to poorer nations to put people to work.
  Robert Reich
  Labor Secretary

The ambition of global capitalism is increasingly apparent. It is determined to construct a set of international institutions that will end cultural, national, and political sovereignty. Such institutions will universally govern or act as an oversight body to the market forces of the world. Such institutions will be beholden purely to the interests of global capitalism. Global capitalism wants to use economics to end politics. The goal is to get the world under one system. Economics in the form of global capitalism is seen to have the necessary rigor to develop all of the peoples of the world by ending the tyranny of race, ethnicity, nationality, and so forth. In this regard, besides undermining political and cultural sovereignty, global capitalism also aims to end racial and national sovereignty. Global capitalism wants the world to be subject to the rule and power of market forces. It wants competition to become the order of the world as competition supposedly makes us better human beings by weaning us away from dependency and dysfunctionality. Indeed, global capitalism is deeply appealing to many peoples in developing nations. Its materialism is alluring. Its promise to end various kinds of strife and human misery is also alluring. Indeed, its promise of material prosperity and progress for all peoples is difficult to resist.

We in the U.S. know global capitalism best. We know how global capitalism displaces diversity. We know how global capitalism is bent on maximizing the most amount of order and control on human beings. We know how global capitalism is bent on subordinating human beings to structures, institutions, and laws that delimit human action. We know how global capitalism subordinates human interests to the interests of wealth and power. We can no doubt warn others about how values and beliefs that uphold family, community, and friendship will be subtly replaced by values and beliefs that stress individualism, materialism, and competition. Indeed, global capitalism displaces worldviews and cultures. It also dispossesses us of empathy and compassion. It fosters distrust, suspicion, and selfishness. Survival becomes the primary goal. Global capitalism also encourages us to rapaciously exploit each other and the resources of the world for selfish gain. It strives constantly to attain the most control, the most order, the most exploitation.

Forging A New Understanding Of Progress

We have to ultimately expose the illusion that global capitalism offers the best and only path to progress. Proponents of capitalism successfully get away with casting opponents of global capitalism as being against progress. This ploy always works in the interest of global capitalism. It caricatures opponents as fools and cowards. This strategy makes it difficult to take seriously opponents' concerns and criticisms, especially when the onus is on opponents to unpack complex arguments that in no way lend to nice sound bytes. Opponents are always working uphill.

We will eventually move beyond the tyranny of race, ethnicity, geography, and nationality. Nothing is inherently wrong with this kind of movement. Historically, human beings have always been tearing down the walls of division and fragmentation. This will happen without global capitalism. Abiding and respecting the rhythms and movements of the natural world give us an understanding of progress that spares us the negative outcomes that come with global capitalism. We can have diversity without social devolution, and order without hierarchy. We can also have prosperity without inequality, and coordination without coercion. Natural systems harness all the forces that constitute such systems in ways that make for symmetry and beauty. Progress is of this world. Even without human beings, the world will always move forward.

Natural systems give us an understanding of progress that stresses complexity and harmony. Systems move organically towards increasing levels of complexity. Diversity and homogeneity, order and chaos, disequilibrium and equilibrium, and other dialectical forces work in tandem to increase the complexity of natural systems. Complexity correlates with the vitality of systems. It also correlates with the quality and quantity of relationships with other systems. Systems with high complexity have the most and highest quality relationships with other systems. Quality is assessed in terms of complexity. In other words, a highly complex system is one that is highly connected and integrated. A system that possesses high levels of complexity also reflects high levels of permeability and flexibility. High levels of quantity and quality of relationships make for such attributes because different systems are constantly pushing the system to adjust and respond to all kinds of changes.

Complexity increases access to resources and communication. It exposes systems to new relations that make for the evolution of new ideas, new meanings, new experiences. This kind of evolution expands the ability of systems to respond to changes that come from other systems. It expands options. Complexity also correlates with the integrity of systems. Complex systems are robust and resilient because of the high levels of connection and integration that are the hallmark of such systems. Such systems also tend to act upon the world rather than merely react to changes in the world. In contrast, global capitalism defines progress in terms of simplicity. It wants to strip the world of diversity and mystery. It wants to reduce all of the world to markets and consumers. It wants all peoples to have one set of values, beliefs, truths, hopes, fears, assumptions, and so forth. We are all to want to prosper economically and materially. We are to believe that the world is in conflict with us and that competition rather than cooperation makes for the evolution of good society. Homogeneity derives from simplicity. No doubt, simplicity and homogeneity make for a nice and easy understanding of progress. This understanding makes for good sound bytes. We now pass off simplicity for symmetry and beauty. Supposedly, simplicity is the hallmark of a good explanation.

Global capitalism notions of progress strive in a world that is increasingly divorced from us. We want a world devoid of mystery, ambiguity, and complexity. We have no temperament and currency for explanations that give us no way to control and order the world. Scientism only pretends to want to understand the world. It is really about us projecting our fear of our humanity on the world. It is for this reason that scientism consistently downplays the complexity of the human condition. It only pretends to want to understand what being human really means. Scientism focuses on variables, factors, models, and so forth. We hear about different relationships between variables and the constant testing of different models. We also hear a lot about chimpanzees, apes, and bonoboes. Rarely is any explicit mention made about how a new finding or observation expands our understanding of what being human means. We report findings in relation to other findings and other research. Rarely does any research begin with the stated goal of trying to understand what being human means. We read instead about how the proposed research will test a model, test a relationship, identify a new factor, expand a theory, and so forth. Scientism is bent on creating explanations that are devoid of mystery, ambiguity, and complexity. We are determined to have the world yield to our ambitions. Scientism works in tandem with global capitalism. It is equally bent on simplifying and ordering and controlling the world.

But global capitalism is fraught with many structural problems. It strives on ravaging and plundering the natural resources of the world. But the world can give up only so much resources. Capitalism is also dependent on maximizing order and control of human resources so as to attain maximum profitability. The history of capitalism is one of constantly striving to attain maximum control and order of human beings. All kinds of techniques and practices and arrangements have evolved out of this ambition. Technology continues to be used effectively to this end. It tends to make for a superior kind of disciplining and monitoring of human beings. It is especially productive in keeping labor on tasks. But as capitalism expands and evolves, the demand increases to hold labor cost to a minimum so as to maintain superior competitiveness. This is how technology enters the equation.

Technology offers the most superior way of maintaining

order and control. It has the virtue of being unobtrusive, efficient, and cheap. As such, global capitalism depends increasingly on technology to control labor cost so as to maintain survivability and profitability. The result being the further evolution of technology that is increasingly replacing human beings and contributing to the widening gap between rich and poor. Global capitalism possesses no means to stop these trends. Without the control and order of labor, survivability and profitability are in jeopardy. Labor is therefore destined to disappear in global capitalism. Yet when this happens, that is, when labor disappears, consumers also disappear.

The other structural problem with global capitalism is that the world can only absorb so much materialism. Capitalism demands the constant creation of new markets and consumers. It needs us to constantly want new goods and services. Without this level of consuming, capitalism collapses. In the end, however, human beings can only want and buy so much. Eventually, assuming that the present steep trajectory continues, material saturation will occur and global capitalism will be without new markets and consumers to satisfy.

The Origins of Mutuality

Natural systems give us the hope and potentiality for a society that escapes the contradictions that come with global capitalism. It is mutuality that ultimately makes for the prosperity of any system. In fact, capitalism tends to mask the high levels of mutuality that exist in capitalist systems. We can have mutuality without plundering and ravaging the natural resources of the world. We can attain mutuality without fostering scarcity. The research tells us again and again that most persons prefer cooperation to competition. The reason is obvious: cooperation puts less strain on the human condition. Mutuality complements our need for community, our need for relationships, our need to belong. Individualism rests on many myths. It assumes that human beings have no moral, existential, and spiritual relation to other human beings. It assumes that our power comes from within us. It also assumes that community limits human action. Mutuality rejects such assumptions. It acknowledges that the quality of our humanity correlates with the condition of others' humanity.

Mutuality also recognizes that power resides in our relationships to others. Mutuality enlivens our ability to act upon the world. In addition, mutuality recognizes that trust is an integral component to being human. Human beings strive to trust, want to trust, hope to trust, need to trust. Mutuality rejects the claim that trust evolves out of necessity. It assumes that trust is existential. It is trust, in fact, that distinguishes cooperation from mutuality. We can have cooperation without trust. In most cases, all that is necessary for the evolution of cooperation is the threat of retribution. This threat suffices to keep all sides committed to upholding the agreed upon conditions. But mutuality emphasizes trust rather than retribution. The focus is on deepening the relationships between the different sides. That is, mutuality focuses on building and expanding relationships so as to increase the potentiality of all sides to function and blossom. In this regard, mutuality aspires to transcend differences. It aims to lessen the fear, distrust, and suspicion that is naturally found when different peoples encounter each other. Mutuality moves us towards union. It is therefore inherently nonhierarchical. It organically equalizes the distribution of resources and talents.

We need an emergent ethos that aspires to build mutuality with the different peoples of the world. Mutuality respects the differences of others. It strives for the evolution of all sides as only through such evolution can relationships expand between the different sides. Mutuality views each new relationship as an opportunity to expand the humanity of all sides. Mutuality is a praxis. It is a way of being in the world. The point being that cooperation is elementary. It merely allows us to exist and function. Mutuality, on the other hand, expands our humanity by deepening our understanding of the world. It catalyzes meaning creation. Only mutuality taps our moral, existential, and spiritual strives. It uniquely vitalizes our potentiality.

Democracy and Diversity

Identity politics reinscribes a narrow understanding of democracy. Democracy is a sacred and holy word in U.S. society. It is actually the supposed hallmark of U.S. society—supposedly reflecting all that is uniquely great about this society. It is commonly understood in terms of representation and participation. That is, regardless of race, ethnicity, gender, and class, U.S. society supposedly allows all citizens equal opportunity at participation and representation. Of course we tend to forget that this democracy only recently evolved as for endless decades many citizens had no such opportunity. Still, the U.S. claims purchase on the gospel of democracy and vociferously preaches the gospel to the world. U.S. democracy no doubt has the ability to bring much good to different regions of the world that suppress any kind of participation and representation. Still, to look at democracy purely in terms of participation and representation sustain a narrow and shallow understanding of democracy.

U.S. democracy only pretends to expand human action. In reality, U.S. democracy only fractionally and haphazardly expands human action. Full participation and representation demand the full expansion of the human condition. Our ability to act purposely and deliberately upon the world correlates with the expansion of our humanity. Any system that is committed to obtaining the fullest participation and representation must also be committed to expanding the human condition. Unfortunately, U.S. democracy puts no emphasis on the latter. The reason being that this kind of commitment calls forth the recognition that human beings do have a potentiality that can be enlarged and that this process makes for the betterment of the human condition. Instead, U.S. democracy assumes a deep distrust and suspicion of the human condition. Consequently, rather than putting the focus on the human element, U.S. democracy puts the focus on institutions, structures, and laws. The overarching goal is to delimit human action. That is, U.S. democracy controls rather than expands human action. It only gives us access to a system that is rigidly predetermined. Any discussion about the evolution of this system is off limits. In this way, U.S. democracy ultimately harms the human condition by deliberately blocking its evolution.

A system that focuses on expanding the human condition understands that this expansion will make for its evolution. This expansion will undercut the status quo. This system also acknowledges that this kind of evolution and expansion is vital to its own survival and prosperity. It assumes that evolution is the order of the world. To this end, this system emphasizes practices that foster permeability and flexibility. It puts the focus on enlivening processes, dynamics, and relationships rather than maintaining institutions, structures, and laws. It stresses fluidity rather than rigidity. The goal is to foster environments that foster responsibility and other functional ways of being in the world. A system that acknowledges evolution as the order of the world strives on the interplay between the dialectical forces of the world. Chaos, disequilibrium, conflict, and chaos perform vital functions for the world.

Identity politics makes no demands on U.S. democracy. It merely wants to attain proportional participation and representation for members of historically marginalized and disenfranchised groups. It wants to keep U.S. democracy honest. It wants U.S. democracy to make the necessary alterations and adjustments that will make for the participation and representation of disenfranchised groups. In this regard, identity politics focuses on access issues: voter registration, redrawing of electoral districts to reflect minority populations and districts, fund raising for minority candidates, and lobbying for minority causes. The problem is cast in terms of access. Supposedly, full access will make for a superior democracy by reflecting all the interests and perspectives that the different peoples of this country reflect.

But our reality tells a different story. U.S. democracy is deteriorating rather than improving. Less and less persons are voting and the diversity of the representation is actually lessening with the rise of members from historically marginalized and disenfranchised groups. The supposed inclusion of members of historically disenfranchised groups merely legitimizes a system that serves the interests of others. Of course in most cases such interests harm the interest of disenfranchised groups. Our narrow and shallow understanding of democracy has left us exposed to this kind of mugging of our power. Far from broken, our democracy has been exposed. Getting the money out of the system will do nothing to fix the problem. Adding what now passes for diversity will also do nothing to fix the problem. The deep levels of apathy that now surround the system are a reflection of the alienation that the system fosters by focusing on institutions, structures, and laws. Contrary to theory, U.S. democracy actually thrives on our powerlessness and weakness. It needs us to be dependent and subservient to its institutions, structures, and laws. The goal, after all, is stability and continuity, order and control, so as to maintain the status quo. Evolution supposedly threatens fragmentation and devolution. The new found hegemony that the elites of wealth and power is creating is evolving out of the alienation that our democracy is naturally producing. Consequently, our democracy gives us no mechanisms to stop this hegemony. It is now completely beholden to the interests of this group of elites of wealth and power. Global capitalism uses U.S. democracy as a beachhead to squash other political systems in the world. Pockets of protests in the U.S. will have no effect on stopping global capitalism. This beast gains its power from a system (U.S. democracy) that disempowers and dehumanizes us. Thus, the solution to global capitalism resides in the creation of a system that empowers us, a system that expands our potentiality. We need to begin the push forward for a new conception of democracy that puts the focus on the expansion of the human condition.

We have many local cases of the birthing of this emergent democracy. It is increasingly being practiced in a number of educational, work, and neighborhood environments. These environments are characterized by a consistent set of features that stress collective deliberation and negotiation. We find an emphasis on relationships rather than on structures. The latter, in fact, tend to be nonexistent. This emergent democracy has to be lived and experienced in our everyday habits of being.

VIII
On The Challenge of Diversity
A Case Study

Once again I am dealing with problems of difference. This time, as with too many other times, I am dealing with those who supposedly share my difference, my politics. I am once again to join in a struggle against a racist, sexist, or heterosexist action. I am assumed to be offended. I must therefore sign a petition, write a letter to an editor, demand a sanction, expulsion, or termination, light a candle at a vigil, wear a ribbon, attend a rally, and speak at a Speak Out. I am being subtly pressured to take a moral stand. But I oppose the way the issue is being framed against this latest violation and what is seen as the appropriate course of action. I have no intention of signing any petition, writing any letters, or demanding anyone's expulsion or termination. But my supposedly lack of a visible moral stance is seen as I being complicit in legitimizing the atmosphere for made the offense. There is no openness or willingness to understand my difference, that is, to how I frame, experience, and move in the world. My failure to comply with the demands of the dominant position has once again put me in peril. I am to surrender my difference. But I am unwilling to comply. So once again I am in a fight for my life.

There is always surprise when I announce that I oppose the casting of diversity in terms of race, ethnicity, gender, and sexual orientation. I also oppose the way that minority peoples are increasingly using sensitivity as a weapon against dominant groups by masking the fact that notions like sensitivity, civility, and other such sacred connoting terms, are deeply contested terms. The fact that dominant groups have used civility, such as in the civil rights period, as a means to discipline black and brown peoples, in no way sanctions us to now use sensitivity to discipline dominant groups. This politics is devoid of any virtue. Also, the notion that certain language must be censored, as some language can presumably be psychologically damaging to various peoples, I find dangerous. This position perpetuates the ignorance that meanings reside within language rather than in peoples. It also perpetuates the ignorance that various minority peoples experience the world similarly. In this way this ignorance actually perpetuates an insidious stereotyping. It also undermines communication by overly burdening those who use language with the impossible task of knowing and being responsible for how one's language will be interpreted and experienced. But the matter has now become even more ridiculous, as in those cases where many persons, even prominent scholars, are increasingly insisting that certain language, by merely the way such language sounds and looks, such as the word niggardly, should be banished, although, as in the case of niggardly, the word shares no vocabulary association with nigger. But how can one hope to undermine hegemonies of ignorance with other hegemonies of ignorance?

The problem with this politics of difference is that it perpetuates problematic definitions of diversity by reducing diversity to a noun. It also fails to enlarge our understanding of what being human means and thereby in no enlarges our understanding of what is possible. Further, this politics fails to grasp the inherent human forces that undermine our experiencing and understanding of diversity. It thereby allows us to escape our own many racisms, and the anxieties, insecurities, and paranoia that make for these racisms. In sum, the politics of difference that presumably implicates me because of my own ethnic and racial difference, poses no threat to the status quo. It even legitimizes the status quo by leaving the institutions that perpetuate our own racisms intact. This politics of difference is therefore difficult to escape as every side has a vested interest in its continuity.

But the continuity of this politics diminishes our understanding of diversity and helps perpetuate a worldview that is inherently hostile to diversity. Indeed, what we commonly view as diversity is really plurality. We learn from naturally-occurring ecologies that diversity disrupts, challenges, and makes anew. It pushes ecologies to evolve and flourish. On the other hand, plurality is merely difference that poses no threat to the order of things. It is purely ideological in origin. So whereas naturally-occurring ecologies promote diversity through disruption, evolution, and even revolution, plurality strives for addition, accommodation, and inclusion. Diversity therefore inherently destabilizes the status quo by disrupting and even imploding the foundations that the status quo needs to maintain continuity. Yet only through such disruption ecologies strive and flourish. Diversity is therefore inherently moral. It affirms life. As such, to reduce diversity to a noun, that is, simply something one is as a result of being of a different race, ethnicity, gender, sexual orientation, and so forth, or to reduce the mission of diversity to that of inclusion, is to emasculate and depoliticize diversity and ultimately help perpetuate ideologies and cosmologies that want nothing to do with diversity. Yet minority peoples have, unfortunately, been complicit in perpetuating this reality by failing to interrogate the notion of difference. What we will no doubt find is those of us who are racially, ethnically, and sexually different have the same fears, anxieties, insecurities, and paranoia as others. We too want hierarchy. We too want only so much difference. We therefore want only inclusion as to disrupt the status quo requires us to disrupt our being, that is, to be ready to experience the world differently, that is, to have the courage to rid ourselves of those anxieties, insecurities, and paranoia that paralyze our humanity and put us at each other's throats.

Protests, Petitions, and Vigils

Ever so often a diversity dispute will erupt on a university campus. Chancellors will issue announcements condemning the culpable action and calling for healing, task forces will be assembled to find ways to stop further occurrences of such events, classes will be stopped for teach-ins, speak outs will be organized, vigils will be had and candles lit, and many instructors and students will take the opportunity to publicly chastise the university's administration for failing to do more to make the university safe for minority persons.

We attended the forums last week during which the university community expressed outrage about the racist, misogynist, homophobic and other hateful programming of . . . producers. We were dismayed that the larger issues of institutional racism and marginalization remained unaddressed. With disturbing regularity, black students, other students of color, lesbian, gay, bisexual and transgender students, women and people from diverse backgrounds are disrespected, discouraged and otherwise discriminated against in classrooms and across the campus. This reveals the broad failure of the university and its schools, colleges, departments, faculty and administrators to effectively address the educational and ethical demands of incorporating principles of universal human dignity and respect throughout the institution. This failure signifies the lack of commitment beyond the rhetoric of diversity to the reality of doing anti-racist and other anti-subordination work. This work must not be left to a few departments or faculty members to fulfill the obligation of the entire university and all faculty and administrators.

This script plays out regularly at every university. Just recently, for example, I saw this script play out at my university. The offending actions were shows on a student-run television station. The university community quickly erupted. The chancellor, who "is nationally known as an advocate for affirmative action and for racial and ethnic diversity in higher education," immediately shut down the television station and put out a series of statements denouncing the broadcast and justifying why the station was shut down. She said that the broadcasts were "degrading and divisive." She was also afraid that the broadcasts would "drive a wedge between us in the community" and "divide our community." She promised "to propose avenues for dialogue across what appears to be intractable boundaries among us." The customary task forces were formed, in this case the *Task Force for Institutional Culture*, "to start the hard work of creating new campus culture of inclusion," and the highest ranking minority administrators were pressed into service to head various task forces. The university also made counselors available to help students cope with the "psychological impact" of the broadcasts.

But this time many instructors, students, and alumni, though acknowledging that the broadcasts were crude and offensive, vigorously protested the chancellor's decision to shut down the television station without due process. Most of the faculty in the school of journalism and broadcasting took out a full-page ad in the university's paper criticizing the chancellor for undermining First Amendment guarantees at the university. Articles written by instructors and alumni appeared in the local paper and the controversy even made its way into a column by a nationally syndicated columnist. For many weeks the school newspaper was full of letters either criticizing or defending the chancellor's decision to shut down the television station. The chancellor was forced to put out subsequent statements where she spoke of the challenge of "building an inclusive community," "affirming the rules of acceptable conduct," and "creating a new campus culture of inclusion."

There has been much talk of late about how important it is to preserve the free exchange of ideas—the representation of our academic freedoms to express and debate diverse views and opinions and tastes and values. This is surely critical to all that universities stand for in our educational and discovery mission.

However, I would argue that, in making those freedoms a reality, it is critical that we all come together and agree to abide by rules of civil conduct and exchange, rules that preserve a level playing field of safety and participation for all members of the campus community. We have to take seriously that social fabric—or only some will reap the benefits of "freedom."

In one forum where even standing room was unavailable, one philosophy instructor, whose "areas of expertise are language, hate speech and regulations of language," said "We have to distinguish between speech that is harmful and speech that is merely offensive." The difference between the two, according to the instructor, is that harmful speech can lead to psychological or physical damage. Another instructor from the Writing Program, said that though she was once censored, she supported the chancellor's decision to shut down the television station. "As a writer who has been censored, I can say I wholeheartedly support the chancellor's positions on this situation." The two instructors who were coordinator's of the university's Diversity Initiative, one from the philosophy department and the other from the linguistics department, wrote a letter supporting the chancellor's decision.

The problem with the discourse of censorship is that it acts as if only one sort of harm counts, and all other sorts of harms can be and should be ignored. We would also argue that, in fact, the issue of censorship does not apply to this case. Censorship concerns the restriction of political ideas, but people's concerns about censorship are being used here to protect offensive humor. And the humor in question will in no way widen the scope of our political debate, advance anyone's political understandings or ensure the protection of minority opinion. Quite the reverse. This humor exhibits a caustic unconcern too often found among social elites about the historical and present-day injustice of non-elites. In plain fact, we have here a case where the very privileged in our community are asserting their inalienable rights to use our publicly shared airwaves to demean people from marginalized groups. We hope the community will join the chancellor in insisting that these are not the only rights at issue in this case, and that, when these rights threaten the rights of others, especially the rights of marginalized groups, they are not inalienable.

But many other faculty, students, and alumni were adamant that the chancellor's decision was more egregious as she, in violating the guarantees of the First Amendment, ultimately undermined the safeguards of a democratic society.

In a democratic society, it is not an option to close down the press because of disgust with the content of an entertaining program. Then we silence voices that fulfill their highest calling by exposing our society's ills.

That surely raises the threat of a chilling effect on the other student media—those that report news and those that create entertainment—and on all of us who might silence ourselves for fear of reprisals.

We strongly believe that, in the future, student groups contributing to our campus dialogue must be permitted to make their own successes and mistakes and then deal with the consequences through the established judicial process. The University need not, and should not, put itself in the position of refereeing the content of student speech. The best course is almost always answering speech with more speech, not with enforced silence.

But once again I was dismayed with how one of these diversity eruptions was framed and handled. There was no space for any view that was different to either side of this controversy. Both sides constructed the controversy in such a way that posed no threat to the status quo. But, in my view, the real issue deals with what is the mission of a university in the making of a humane society, and how does a university engage such a mission. I always assumed that the mission of the university is to engage ignorance. This mission assumes that education constitutes a more heuristic approach to ignorance to that of aggression. It also assumes that the goal of education is to interrogate, probe, examine, challenge, and propose. As such, education reckons with the important relationship between ontology, epistemology, and axiology, that is, how our ways of experiencing the world shape our understanding of the world. In short, nothing escapes history. So no construct has a stable meaning. The goal of education is to expose the forces that suppress the evolution of other meanings. It also probes the implications and consequences that come with different meanings and interpretations. But in this controversy at my university this mission was undercut. The university succumbed to aggression. It was no doubt afraid of the matter exploding further and the administration accused of being complicit by failing to take decisive and early action. So the chancellor immediately and unilaterally shut down the television station and made the customary calls for healing and unity. But these actions, unfortunately, do nothing for the university's goal of lessening "the intractable boundaries between us." In fact, these actions egregiously violate the mission of education.

Ignorance will often manifest itself in the most ugly of ways. It will even often wound us as we grapple to subdue it. Most times we will even fail in subduing it. It will torment and frustrate us to no end. But we have no choice but to continue to engage it as the other option is aggression. So yes, I understand the impulse to often forsake education and revert to aggression. But ultimately aggression will only incite aggression and make for a destructive spiral of violence. We will eventually have to return to education or simply face destruction. So outside of some miraculous intervention, education constitutes our most heuristic path to a humane society. Yet the pursuit of education cannot be planned or limited. We have to be ready and willing to go where the pursuit takes us. But of course the ignorance we are really grappling with is our own ignorance, that is, our own anxieties, insecurities, and paranoia that impede our ability to experience and frame the world in more expansive and imaginative ways. Thus what makes education such a fundamental human challenge is that it requires courage— the courage to challenge, probe, and interrupt our own humanity, and to do so honestly and openly.

In this controversy at my university courage was absent. No side was willing or capable of framing the matter beyond free speech. But framing the matter in this narrow way in no way helps us to appreciate the forces and impulses that heighten our fears of each other and also make us brutalize each other. These forces and impulses are originating from outside the university. In other words, the incident at my university cannot be separated from those cosmologies and ideologies that shape the society that locates my university. We therefore cannot separate the controversy from the widening gap between rich and poor, to the unparallel incarceration of persons of color, to the increasing loss of support for those who are most weak and vulnerable, to the increasing rise of social isolation, to the increasing loss of social capital, and to our reckless plundering of the planet's natural resources for selfish gain. Neither can we hope to have an inclusive university community outside of ending these trends. But no statements will be made by my chancellor in regards to reports about incarceration rates continuing to surpass record levels, or about the loss of funding for Head Start, or the widening gap between rich and poor, or about retribution being foundational to our systems of justice. No statements will also be forthcoming on reparations, and no vigils and Speak Outs will be had for the increasing number of children who go without medical insurance in the richest country in the world, or the mothers who are constituting the fastest growing segment of the prison population. I will also never read that my chancellor is a nationally recognized voice for reparations. But no side wants such a larger framing of the controversy as our own complicity will become apparent. However, any solution that neglects this larger context is really no solution at all.

Education will never give us easy and complete solutions.

The world is simply too complex for such solutions. Instead, education will give us options and, in so doing, remind us that the world is laden with possibility. On the other hand, when education is undercut, options disappear and a world with limited possibilities appear. So by undercutting education in this controversy, what emerges are a set of limited options in resolving the controversy. For example, many instructors and students demand that university hire more minority faculty and do a better job of making minorities feel welcome. But these proposed solutions pose no threat to the status quo. Inclusion remains the primary goal—the making of an inclusive university community. But how did inclusion come to be the goal? Or, why is inclusion casually assumed to be the goal of diversity?

No naturally occurring ecology achieves diversity through inclusion. Instead, diversity is achieved through disruption, evolution, and revolution. It emerges by fundamentally disrupting the status quo. In fact, inclusion has no theoretical foundation. It is an ideological notion. However, when we fail to interrogate, which is what happens when education is undercut, we leave intact an ideology that creates, perpetuates, and profits from this notion. But this is also the same ideology that is making for the increasing militarization of our society, the widening gap between rich and poor, the unparallel incarceration of poor people and people of color, and our reckless plundering of the planet's natural resources. This is the ideology of hierarchy, the ideology of retribution, the ideology of survival of the fittest. This is the ideology that begins on the premise that human beings are by nature beasts and savages who need hierarchy in order to attain progress and moral evolution. This is also the ideology that assumes that there is an inherent and intractable conflict between the world and us. This is therefore the ideology that makes believe that our prosperity is dependent on us developing the means—as in our sciences and technologies—to win this conflict against a world that is hostile to our prosperity. In sum, this is the ideology that instills in us a deep suspicion of the world, each other, and our own humanity. Therefore in every way this ideology undermines the conditions that are vital for diversity to flourish. For what diversity requires most is a belief that the world is pregnant with possibility. It also requires us to believe that there is no intractable and inherent conflict between the world and us, and that human beings possess a potentiality that allows us to escape hierarchy.

But these beliefs speak to a different ideology as none of these beliefs can be woven into our current ideology. Our current ideology will forever remain hostile to diversity, which is to say that inclusion will remain the stated goal, thereby allowing us to engage in the illusion that through censorship we can achieve an inclusive community. But inclusion, in being devoid of any rigorous theoretical foundation, constitutes a highly dangerous ideological notion. It requires that we assimilate and tolerate each other's differences. But nothing is heuristic about either of these approaches and neither pushes us to engage and challenge the different histories and ontologies that make for our differences. Also, neither challenges us to interrogate that which wants our inclusion. With inclusion therefore come other theoretically challenged notions, such as toleration and assimilation. But increasingly the most dangerous notions that come with inclusion are those of sensitivity and civility. These notions are purely ideological in origin, which is also to say that both concepts are inherently reactionary as what one person may find offensive is always likely to be different from what others find offensive. Yet there is no ideologically neutral way of determining which definition of sensitivity and civility should prevail. Ultimately, sensitivity and civility demand nothing much from us. That is, nether demands any disruption in our worldview nor any reallocation of resources and opportunities. In this way, neither poses a threat to the status quo. Historically marginalized and disenfranchised peoples therefore gain nothing from the promotion of sensitivity and civility. These concepts work in tandem to block interrogation of larger ideological apparatuses that put us at the throats of each other. But again, when inclusion is the stated goal, sensitivity and civility will the best that will be had.

Inclusion will also give us affirmative action and this too poses no threat to the status quo. Indeed, in case after case that is made for affirmative action, the underlying message is always that it poses no threat to the status quo and that its benefits outweigh its costs. In fact, affirmative action is cast as being good for the status quo—a win/win arrangement. For example, in various writings about affirmative action and the "need to defend diversity," my chancellor, who was provost at Michigan University during that university's famous affirmative action legal challenges, claims that diversity enriches the learning environment by encouraging "us to pay attention, to see ourselves and the world in a slightly new light." It also promotes "cognitive challenges and stellar performances." But most of all, the diversity that affirmative action promotes helps "to construct environments for inter-group relations that pave the way for racial integration—for living and working harmoniously together across the lines of race." Indeed, "Our need to consider the nation's compelling interest in affirmative action turned our attention squarely to its benefits, which include drawing on a full talent pool in ways that broaden the opportunities for social/economic mobility for more Americans. By bringing a more diverse group of students to campus, we are in the position to educate all students in an environment where they will be challenged to see new possibilities for themselves and their world because of the mix of voices and perspectives at the table. Hardest of all, but most significantly, these experiences will, as they become more numerous, ultimately prepare all students to live and work in harmony in a multiracial society."

These are no doubt quite noble objectives. In fact, when cast this way how could anyone oppose affirmative action? Even Justice Sandra Day O'Connor acknowledges that diversity—which affirmative action cultivates—"promotes learning outcomes and better prepares students for an increasingly diverse workforce, for society, and the legal profession." But does affirmative action promote justice? Does it cultivate diversity? Does it constitute a decent redress for over 350 years of slavery and Jim Crow? To every question, the answer is No. There is no affirmative action in naturally-occurring ecologies. Affirmative action emerges when destruction of the status quo is seen as a non-option.

But how did certain peoples come to have the power to dictate what options are legitimate and illegitimate? How did these peoples achieve this power and privilege? Also, how do these peoples preserve this power? These are the important questions that affirmative action blocks. Still, affirmative action affords no diversity as diversity is always emergent. It can never be hierarchically imposed on an ecology. This means that no ecology can hierarchically limit diversity. If an ecology attempts to do so it will simply perish. Yet this is exactly what affirmative action does. It aims to limit diversity—and thereby protect the status quo—by reducing diversity to a noun.

But peoples who have been historically marginalized, disenfranchised, and brutalized win hardly anything from affirmative action as such practices only allow for inclusion into systems that originally made for the oppression of such peoples and are still making for the oppression of others. Moreover, affirmative action does nothing to stop the widening gap between rich and poor, the increasing incarceration of persons of color, our escalating destruction of the planet, and so forth. Nevertheless, affirmative action makes for the impression that minority peoples are generously being given valuable opportunities and resources by morally upstanding and progressive members of dominant groups. In reality, however, affirmative action in no way makes up for the misery that most minority peoples have suffered. It also undercuts any serious discussion of reparations by making reparations seem like a foolish and outlandish demand. In this way, affirmative action and the goal of inclusion push historically marginalized peoples to limit history, to function in the world as ahistorical beings, and to lose sight of the historical processes that made for a society that now enjoys the power and moral suasion to cast reparations as a foolish and outlandish demand for over 350 years of slavery and Jim Crow.

The success of this foregoing of history is seen in the increasing conservatism of minority politics, such as in our support of the death penalty, support for legislation that increases our incarceration, support for affirmative action rather than reparations, and our support for candidates who maintain the status quo. It is also seen in our rampant materialism and consumerism, and the loss of a liberation theology for a theology of individual redemption. In other words, by removing history from the equation, inclusion has depoliticized race and ethnicity. Now both are simply colors in a rainbow. Such is the emasculation that inclusion demands. But when history is lost, as in this case, what is also lost is our humanity as history anchors us in the world. It gives us a moral direction by obligating us to end the conditions that made for our forefathers and foremothers' oppression. Thus peoples who are without history are ripe for further subjugation and oppression.

Final Thoughts

So I want nothing to do with inclusion and affirmative action or with sensitivity and civility. This includes wanting nothing to do with the latest full page statement that was sponsored by faculty in Women's Studies, African American Studies, Latino-Latin Studies, Native Studies, and LGBT Studies, that claims that the chancellor is "a strong leader committed to the deepest principles of a multicultural society" and that I "applaud ... her courageous stand against racism, sexism, heterosexism, ability-ism, and all forms of discrimination." It is simply hard to believe that by simply shutting down a student—run television station one has shown to be "committed to the deepest principles of a multicultural society" and demonstrated to be "courageous." How did the bar become so low?

I want justice. That is, I want the end of hierarchy, the end of arrangements that undercut the natural rhythms of evolution, disruption, and revolution. I want arrangements that would allow our potentiality to flourish and make for worlds that are overflowing with possibility. I want such arrangements for all peoples as my liberation is entwined with the liberation of others. So though race and ethnicity are my location, neither is my destination. I am a being who belongs to the world. How the world goes so I go.

I therefore cannot separate my well-being from the condition of the world. But this is the definitive struggle, especially for peoples who have been historically marginalized and disenfranchised. On one hand, I must join in the struggle that comes with being a minority, and thereby align myself with such peoples. Yet I must simultaneously function as a human being who belongs to the world, and thereby is beyond my race and ethnicity. The struggle is by no means contradictory. In fact, I cannot successfully do one without the other. The latter allows me a larger view of things and a better understanding of what is ultimately at stake. On the other hand, my race and ethnicity give me a location and point of action within the larger struggle. The problem arises when we lose sight of the larger struggle. When we do so we lose sight of what is really at stake. We also lose the ability to cast our struggle within a larger backdrop. In short, we become myopic, and thereby no better than those who subjugate us. But our myopia only serves to mask our own complicit in much of own division and subjugation. For how can one really separate discussions of race and ethnicity from, for example, discussions of the planet's degradation resulting from our reckless plundering of the planet's natural resources? Yet this is exactly what has been achieved, and one need look no further than how discussions of diversity on US campuses are framed again and again to recognize this tragic reality.

Epilogue

I have sought to show that identity politics harms our understanding of diversity. It legitimizes the politics of the status quo by drawing upon many of the bedrock assumptions that the status quo uses to maintain fragmentation and separation. In so doing, identity politics poses no threat to the status quo. Its aim is purely inclusion. Yet no real inclusion can occur without a politics that ends fragmentation and separation. Any politics that maintains separation and fragmentation will always foster exclusion. We will always find practices that harm the evolution of diversity, mutuality, and equality. We will find hierarchy.

But hierarchy harms the human condition. It thwarts the evolution of our moral, existential, and spiritual potentiality. It blocks our questing for deep meanings and thereby our ability to come to communion with the world. In this way, besides cheapening our understanding of diversity and relegitimizing the status quo, identity politics ultimately harms the human condition. It contributes to the distortion of what being human. This distortion undermines our ability to act purposely upon the world by reifying the notion that our contemporary reality is supposedly the best that is humanly possible. That is, this distortion subordinates us to the hopes and fears of the status quo. It subtly and perniciously disciplines our ways of being in the world. Further, identity politics distorts our understanding of the world. It perpetuates the notion that the world is in conflict with us and us in conflict with the world. As a result, it reaffirms a hostile orientation to the world. Most of all, identity politics helps mask the fallout that is emerging from the status quo. It turns us away from the unparallel levels of mental sickness and human despair, the growing disparity in wealth distribution, the collapsing of the planet from our unrelenting plundering of the world's natural resources, and the increasing rise of a market consciousness that further threatens to stop the necessary distribution of resources that are vital to help all human beings have productive and healthy lives. Identity politics falsely assumes that such problems have a different set of origins, thus needing a different set of solutions and advocates. But of course nothing could be further from the truth. All human problems have origins in fragmentation and separation, and, as such, can only find remedy in union and communion.

But the status quo is us. We are all making for the perilous condition of the world. It is our own hopes and fears that give legitimacy to the status quo. It is our own selfishness that makes for the growing wealth disparity between rich and poor. It is our own apathy that makes for human misery and human despair. It is our own distrust and suspicion of our humanity that make for the fragmentation that pervades the world. The racism, sexism, heterosexism, and classism that are found in the world belong to all of us. We wish to risk no life. This is why identity politics poses no threat to the status quo. To look at others differently requires a willingness to first look at ourselves differently. But we are captured by our fears.

We have consistently behaved badly. We have even persecuted and killed our prophets. We are by no means without sin. Still, the notion of all revolutions being local works. It reminds us that revolutions have to begin with us. Revolutions have to be lived. This is what our many prophets teach us. The notion of all revolutions being local reminds us of the tribulations that come with forging new habits of being. It also forces us to understand what is exactly being required of others and ourselves, and, as a result, expands our humanity by deepening our empathy and compassion for the struggles that we and others must engage so to help realize a world that is always promoting new and different ways of experiencing the world.

References

Arnett, R. C. (1986). *Communication and community: Implications of Martin's Buber dialogue.* Carbondale, IL: Southern Illinois University Press.

Arthos, J. (2000). Who are we and who am I? Gadamer's communal ontology as palimpsest. *Communication Studies, 51*, 15-34.

Bateson, M. C. (1994). *Peripheral visions.* New York: HarperCollins.

Belay, G. (1993). Toward a paradigm shift for intercultural and international communication:

New research directions. *Communication Yearbook, 16*, 437-457.

Buber, M. (1970). *I and thou.* New York: Scribner.

Buber, M. (1994). Genuine dialogue and the possibilities of peace. In R. Anderson, K. Cissna, & R. Arnett (Eds.) *The reach of dialogue: Confirmation, voice, and community* (pp. 306-312). Cresskill, NJ: Hampton.

Capra, F. (1983). *The turning point: Science, society and the rising culture.* New York: Bantam Books.

Casmir, F. L. (1993). Third-culture building: A paradigm shift for international and intercultural communication. *Communication Yearbook, 16*, 407-428.

Chen, G., & Starosta, W. J. (1996). Intercultural communication competence: A synthesis. *Communication

Yearbook. 19, 353-383.

Chong-Yeong, L. (2003). Language and human rights. *Journal of Intergroup Relations, 29* (3), 57-65.

Cissna, K. C., & Anderson, R. (1994). Communication and the ground of dialogue. In R. Anderson, K. Cissna, & R. Arnett (Eds.), *The reach of dialogue: Confirmation, voice, and community* (pp. 9-30). Cresskill, NJ: Hampton.

Cottone, L. P. (1993). The perturbing worldview of chaos: Implications for public relations. *Public Relations Review, 19*, 167-176.

Czubaroff, J., & Friedman, M. (2000). A conversation with Maurice Friedman. Southern *Communication Journal, 65*, 243-254.

Deetz, S. (1995). *Transforming communication, transforming business.* Cresskill, NJ: Hampton.

Dervin, B. (1991). Comparative theory reconceptualized: From entities and states to processes and dynamics. *Communication Theory, 1*, 59-69.

Fogel, A. (1993). *Developing through relationships.* Chicago: University of Chicago Press.

Freire, P. (1993). *Pedagogy of the oppressed.* New York: Continuum.

Fry, K. G. (1998). A cultural geography of Lake Wobegon. *Howard Journal of Communications, 9*, 303-322.

Gonzalez Echevarría, R. (1997, March 29). *Is "Spanglish" a language?* New York Times, A. 29.

Gordon, R. D. (2000). Karl Jaspers: Existential philosopher of dialogical communication. *Southern Communication Journal, 65*, 105-117.

Gribbin, J. (1984). *In search of Schroedinger's cat: Quantum Physics and reality*. New York: Bantam Books.

Herbert, N. (1987). *Quantum reality: Beyond the new physics*. New York: Anchor Books.

Huntington, S. (2004). *Who are we? The challenges to America's national identity*. New York: Simon & Schuster.

Iyer, P. (2000). *The global soul: Jet lag, shopping malls, and the search for home*. New York: Knopf.

Jantsch, E. (1980). *The self-organizing universe*. Oxford: Pergamon Press.

Kong, D. (2003, June 14). Hybrid theory. *Pocho.com*. http://www.pocho.com/news/2002/spanglish/spanglishstory.html

Lee, W. S., Wang, J., Chung, J., & Hertel, E. (1995). A sociohistorical approach to intercultural communication. *Howard Journal of Communications, 6*, 262-291.

Martin, J., & Nakayama, T. K. (1999). Thinking dialectically about culture and communication. *Communication Theory, 9*, 1-25.

McPhail, M. L. (1996). *Zen in the art of rhetoric*. New York: State University of New York Press.

Moon, D. G. (1996). Concepts of culture: Implications for intercultural communication research. *Communication Quarterly, 44*, 70-84.

Morales, E. (2002). *Living in Spanglish: The search for Latino identity in America*. NewYork: St. Martin's Griffin.

Murphy, P. (1996). Chaos theory as a model for managing issues and crises. *Public Relations Review, 22*, 95-113.

Murray, J. W. (2000). Bakhtinian answerability and Levinasian responsibility: Forging a fuller dialogical communicative ethics. *Southern Communication Journal, 65*, 133-150.

Olmsted, A. P. (1998). Words are acts: Critical race theory

as a rhetorical construct. *Howard Journal of Communications, 9*, 323-332.

Pearce, W. B., & Littlejohn, S. W. (1997). *Moral conflict: When social worlds collide.* Thousands Oak, CA: Sage.

Prigogine, I. & Stengers, I. (1984). *Order out of chaos.* New York: Bantam Books.

Rodriguez, A. (2003). *Diversity as liberation (II): Introducing a new understanding of diversity.* Cresskill, NJ: Hampton.

Rodriguez, R. (2002). *Brown: The last discovery of America.* New York: Penguin.

Said, E. (2001, 16 September). *Islam and the West are inadequate banners.* TheObserver (http://www.observer.co.uk/comment/story)

Said, E. (2000). Reflections on exile and other essays. Cambridge, MA: Harvard University.

Seeger, M., Sellnow, T. L., & Ulmer, R. R. (1998). Communication, organization, and crisis. *Communication Yearbook, 21*, 231-275.

Shotter, J. (2000). Inside dialogical realities: From an abstract-systematic to a participatory-wholistic understanding of communication. *Southern Communication Journal, 65*, 119-132.

Shutter, R. (1993). On third-culture building. *Communication Yearbook, 16*, 429-436.

Starosta, W. (1991, May). *Third culture building: Chronological development and the role of third parties.* Paper presented at the annual meeting of the International Communication Association, Chicago, IL.

Stavans, I. (2000a). Spanglish: Tickling the tongue. *World Literature Today, 74*, 555-558.

Stavans, I. (2000b, October 13). *The gravitas of Spanglish.* Chronicle of Higher Education. http://chronicle.com/free/v47/i07/07b00701.htm

Thayer, L. (1995). *Pieces: Towards a revisioning of communication/life.* Greenwich, CT: Ablex.

Weinberg, S. (1995, October 5). *Reductionism redux.* The New York Review of Books, pp. 1-6.

Weinberg, S. (2001, May 31). *Can science explain everything? Anything?* The New York Review of Books, pp. 1-9.

Witte, K., Meyer, G., Bidol, H., Casey, M. K., Kopfman, J., Maduschke, K., Marshall, A., Morrison, K., Ribisl, K. M., & Robbins, S. (1996). Bringing order to chaos: A health communication model. *Communication Studies, 47*, 229-242.

Véliz, C. (1994). *The new world and the gothic fox: Culture and economy in English and Spanish America.* Berkeley, CA: University of California Press.

Printed in the United States
83354LV00002B/82-174/A